THE CHURCH, WOMEN BISHOPS AND PROVISION

THE INTEGRITY OF ORTHODOX OBJECTIONS TO THE PROPOSED LEGISLATION ALLOWING WOMEN BISHOPS

CONTRIBUTORS:

ROGER BECKWITH, SARAH FINCH, CHARLES RAVEN, VINAY SAMUEL AND CHRIS SUGDEN

WITH AN INTRODUCTION AND A CONCLUSION BY PHILIP GIDDINGS

AND APPENDICES BY:

MICHAEL OVEY, VINAY SAMUEL AND ANTHONY THISELTON

The Latimer Trust

The Church, Women Bishops and Provision © The Latimer Trust 2011

ISBN 978-0-906327-01-9

Published by The Latimer Trust, November 2011

Cover photograph: © anson tsui – Fotolia.com

The Latimer Trust (formerly Latimer House, Oxford) is a conservative Evangelical research organisation within the Church of England, whose main aim is to promote the history and theology of Anglicanism as understood by those in the Reformed tradition. Interested readers are welcome to consult its website for further details of its many activities.

The Latimer Trust
London N14 4PS UK
Registered Charity: 1084337
Company Number: 4104465
Web: www.latimertrust.org
E-mail: administrator@latimertrust.org

About this book

This book addresses the question why, since the Bible affirms that in Christ 'there is neither male nor female' (Galatians 3:28), those who stress the importance of biblical orthodoxy in church life are objecting to the proposed women bishops legislation.

This symposium was commissioned in November 2010 by a number of members of General Synod – some in favour of women priests and women bishops, some not in favour – who wished to see the theological arguments being more fully explored. They had not been adequately addressed in General Synod debates over the years, as many people have recognized. So this book presents these arguments. It also includes evidence to show that, since the mid-1990s when women were first ordained, the richly varied ministry within the Church of England of women who are not ordained as priests has been growing strongly.

The commissioning group of General Synod members all agree that a proper legal framework should be in place, to provide the security of an ongoing ministry in the Church of England for those who will not be able to accept the ministry of women bishops.

The women bishops legislation, as it stands, does not give proper place to the theological positions contained in this book, positions which have every right to a proper and continued expression in the Church of England. And a 'Code of Practice' on its own will not ensure that there will be proper places in the selection, training and ordination of the next generation of Church of England clergy for those who cannot accept the ministry of women bishops. In short, better, more secure, provision is required.

Some people argue that to make such provision would reduce women bishops to second-class bishops. That criticism relies upon an unbiblical view of 'mono-episcopacy' which, while represented in much (but not all) Church of England practice of episcopacy, fails to take into account the shared leadership that characterizes the New Testament Church.

About the authors

The Revd Dr Roger Beckwith, for many years with Latimer House, is a specialist in Anglican theology.

Mrs Sarah Finch is a member of General Synod.

Dr Philip Giddings is Chairman of the House of Laity of the General Synod.

The Revd Dr Mike Ovey is Principal of Oak Hill Theological College, London and made submissions to the Rochester Report on Women in the Episcopate.

The Revd Charles Raven is Rector of Christ Church Wyre Forest, Kidderminster.

Canon Dr Vinay Samuel is Director of the Oxford Centre for Religion and Public Life.

Canon Dr Chris Sugden is Executive Secretary of Anglican Mainstream and a member of General Synod.

Canon Professor Anthony Thiselton is Emeritus Professor of Christian Theology at the University of Nottingham and was a member of the House of Bishops' Working Party on Women in the Episcopate 2001-2005.

CONTENTS

Introduction

Is there a better way?

As the Church of England discusses, debates and prays about the proposed legislation to allow the consecration of women bishops, it is evident that the form of that legislation is causing some anxiety. That anxiety is not confined to those who are opposed to women bishops in principle; it is shared by some who are in favour – but who do not wish to proceed in a way which would marginalise or unchurch those who are against. These anxieties are mostly focussed on the questions of what 'provision' should be made, and how, for those who cannot in conscience accept this development. A very great deal has been written on the arguments for and against the principle of allowing women bishops. It is not intended to repeat those here. They are judiciously summarised in the Rochester Report, *Women Bishops in the Church of England?*, which analyses the major positions in its fifth chapter under the heading 'Can it be right in principle?'. Anyone interested in this issue, and certainly anyone who has a part to play in the process of deciding whether the proposed legislation should be approved, should read and reflect on that chapter.[1]

Why, therefore, do we need yet more material?

There are two reasons: first, the Church of England is now considering not the principle of having women bishops but actual legislation ('the Draft Measure') – a particular way of providing for women bishops to be appointed. There are strongly-held, contrasting views about how that should be done, especially on what provision should be made for those who cannot in conscience accept it. The Draft Measure provides for a Code of Practice; some would prefer a simple 'one-clause' measure, others would prefer statutory provision for the transfer of oversight. A

---

[1] *Women Bishops in the Church of England?* Published for the House of Bishops of the General Synod of the Church of England by Church House Publishing. Copyright © The Archbishops' Council 2004. The report can be found online at: http://www.churchofengland.org/media/39784/gs1557.pdf

key element in the debate has been, and is, how to hold together as many as possible of these different, and in some cases competing, strands of opinion. So the question to be addressed is not whether there should be a Measure to allow the consecration of women bishops, but whether the present Draft Measure is the best way of doing it: in short, is there a better way?

The second reason is that the important theological issues involved in the argument about the principle of allowing women bishops have also to be engaged with when considering the different ways of actually doing it. Some of the anxieties which the argument of this book seeks to express arise from the conviction that the theological issues, particularly those about our understanding of the nature of the church and of authority, have not been adequately addressed when the draft legislation was being considered. Underlying this are two concerns: first, not to jettison the distinctive ethos of Anglicanism which currently combines a plurality of traditions; and, second, to ensure that those who have faithfully ministered, and been ministered to, within the Church of England from within those traditions can continue to do so in good conscience, rather than being marginalised or excluded.

What the draft legislation proposes

The Draft Measure now being considered in dioceses and deaneries has six main elements. These are:

- to permit the consecration of women as bishops and the continued ordination of women to the priesthood

- to repeal the 1993 legislation which provided for the ordination of women to the priesthood with arrangements for 'opting out'

- to oblige diocesan bishops to have a scheme for delegating episcopal ministry to a male bishop

- to entitle a parish to issue a 'letter of request' to the diocesan bishop seeking the ministry of a male bishop

- to entitle a parish to issue a 'letter of request during a vacancy' to the diocesan bishop requesting a male priest to be appointed

- to require the House of Bishops to draw up a Code of Practice, to be approved by the General Synod

Who is this book for?

It is not primarily for those unable to accept the ministry of women bishops: these Anglicans are probably already convinced of the trend of argument in these pages. Nor is it intended to 'convert' those who are strong advocates of allowing women bishops – 'Let's just get on with it!' Rather, it is for those who are in favour of the principle, yet hesitate about the way in which it is being done. This book is designed to show good theological grounds for the Church of England seeking a better way of allowing women bishops than the Draft Measure currently offers. And we also believe that, whether we are for or against in principle, addressing these issues and reflecting together on the questions of authority and church order will enrich us all. If we could get this right, and avoid the distracting arguments dragging on – and also avoid the alienation that would follow the legislation if passed in its present form – we would have the opportunity as a church to turn our full attention to those pressing issues of mission and evangelism, and fulfil our vocation to be the church for all the people of this land.

That line of reasoning led to this symposium being commissioned in November 2010 by a number of members of General Synod, some in favour of women priests and women bishops, and some not, but who all wished that the theological arguments should be properly explored. Those who commissioned the symposium agree that a robust legal framework should be in place, to maintain the security of an ongoing ministry, within the Church of England, for those who will be unable to accept the ministry of women bishops. They do not accept that the discretionary Code of Practice offered in the Draft Measure will be sufficient; it will not be able to guarantee provision for the selection, training and ordination of the future generations of Church of England clergy unable to accept the ministry of women bishops.

What theological issues still need to be settled?

Although the General Synod approved legislation to allow women priests almost twenty years ago, debate about the acceptability of that development has continued. Amongst Evangelicals two organizations – AWESOME (Anglican Women Evangelicals: Supporting our Ordained Ministry) and Reform – have recently held a series of three consultations on the issues.[2] In a joint statement at the end of those consultations they highlighted the key areas in which ongoing discussion among Evangelicals continues to be required:

- the effect on **biblical interpretation** of different understandings of the relationship between exegesis of specific texts in their original contexts, wider biblical theology, and the role of doctrine and systematic theology

- the form and significance of **creation order** in relation to being made male and female, especially as revealed in Genesis 2 and later biblical appeals to it.

- the doctrine of **the Trinity**, in particular whether or not language of submission and obedience is to be used for the eternal intra-Trinitarian relationship of the Son to the Father and the significance of any such order within the Trinity for the ordering of relationships between men and women in the church and husband and wife in marriage

- the relationship between **submission and obedience** and whether there is a universal Christ-like mutual submission among Christians or a specific submission of wives to husbands whose position as head is to be understood in terms of Christ-like authority

- the connection between any ordering in **relationship between husband and wife** and any ordering of men and women within the ministries and offices of the church

- the nature of **episcopal jurisdiction** and the provision therefore required for evangelicals opposed to women bishops when women become bishops

The contributions brought together in this book provide one response to that call. They engage with the arguments advanced on both sides of the case. As our purpose is not to argue against those who are in favour of women bishops, but rather to urge that proper provision be made for those who have principled objections, it is necessary to establish that 'principled objections' are theologically well-grounded and consonant

---

[2] The papers discussed at each of the three consultations are available at http://www.awesome.org.uk/?page_id=607

with the ethos and historic formularies of the Church of England. Recognising that there are such objections is not, of course, the same as agreeing with them.

Plan of the book

In the five chapters and three appendices which follow we offer reasoned arguments for the proposition that there must a better way forward than the current Draft Measure. Thus in *Chapter 1* we address the key issues of **order, equality and culture** through the lens of the relationship of 'Church' and 'Kingdom'. It argues that applying the verse '[in Christ] there is neither male nor female' (Galatians 3:28, ESV) to matters of church order is to misapply Scripture. The better guide to the reality of the Kingdom is to be found in the New Testament teaching on marriage, which draws on an asymmetrical understanding of equality and, echoing the order of the Trinity and creation, crucially distinguishes between the authority of direction and the authority of domination.

In the following three chapters those arguments are pursued at greater depth as we consider the meaning of **fairness and justice, the issue of mutuality and the implementation of 'reception'**.

Chapter 2 addresses two questions: first, how we are to understand human identity in the light of Scripture? Here we challenge the utopian and **rationalist premises** underlying contemporary feminist arguments and the claim that the Holy Spirit has allowed to the church to continue in what, on feminist arguments, is fundamental error for so long. Secondly, this chapter critiques the argument advanced by proponents of the proposed legislation for rescinding the accommodation of the 'two integrities' established by the 1993 Act of Synod – thereby going back on the **solemn promises** made at the time. The case for rescission is based on secular understandings of the concepts of gender and rights which, it is argued here, are contrary to the Judaeo-Christian tradition. The biblical understanding is that gender is an essential not accidental feature of human identity, and that human freedom flows from mutuality of relationships rather than autonomy.

In *Chapter 3* the theme of mutuality of relationships is developed further as we explore in greater depth the creative interplay of **gender equality and difference** which we find in the New Testament. This involves, first of all, grappling with **hermeneutics** – that is, the question of whether we are reading Scripture correctly: how do we decide what is of universal application and what is only local? So here we make a careful examination of the New Testament teaching on 'headship' in the light of the arguments drawing on cultural context. Second, it involves grappling with **Christology** – that is, how we understand the actual human nature of Jesus Christ, the Second Person of the Trinity, truly human and truly divine. So here we consider the implications of the significance of gender difference for our understanding of the identity of Jesus of Nazareth – a point already taken by some feminist theologians who argue for the need to reinterpret Christ as 'Christa'. If that is a step too far, how far can we legitimately go? Should we, for example, agree with Bonhoeffer[3] that the result of liberal theology is that, by passing over the manhood of Jesus, we bring Him more than ever into the field of speculation and reconstruction?

The arguments addressed in Chapter 3 illustrate that historically the Church has had to resolve disputes about the basis for belief as well as about the content of that belief. That in turn raises the question which we consider in *Chapter 4*: how does and should the Church decide those disputes? In our current context this means: **how do we recognize what should be received and what should be rejected – the issue of Reception?** The Church of England claims to be both Catholic and Reformed, in continuity with the Universal Church reaching back to the time of the Ecumenical Creeds of the fourth and fifth centuries. Historically, that claim has rested on a commitment to Reception, a process of discerning what is in accord with what has already been given, supremely through the Scriptures. In this Chapter we examine the implications of that understanding of Reception for the decision-making processes of the Church of England, and the Anglican Communion, since the decision to go ahead with women's ordination to the priesthood. It is argued here that the process of 'Open Reception' has become a route to experimentation, and therefore radical discontinuity with the received tradition and the voice of Scripture rather than to faithful continuity with it. Since few want to argue that there should be no boundaries at all, what is the remedy for this excessive malleability of teaching and practice? The answer we suggest is to re-visit and apply the Church of England's own Articles and

---

[3]   Dietrich Bonhoeffer, *Christology*, (Collins, 1966), p.83-4.

Canons, specifically Articles XX, XXI and XXXIV and Canon A5 which provide for legitimate diversity which takes account of different cultural contexts within the boundary that 'nothing be ordained against God's Word'.

Does that line of argument mean no change or development is possible? To demonstrate the contrary we set out in *Chapter 5* some arguments for a different way of **developing women's ministry**, a way adopted by a number of local churches who could not go along with the General Synod 1992 decision to ordain women to the priesthood/presbyterate. These arguments seek to build on the complementarity of functions and roles of men and women set out in Scripture and to model a collaborative partnership in church leadership. To underpin these arguments, and demonstrate that they are not just theoretical, we present research findings reporting the experience of men and women involved in some of the local churches who have taken this route, which they consider offers a better way ahead.

It is the principal purpose of this book to set out in some depth the key issues which the Church of England needs to address, at the time when the Draft Measure to allow the consecration of women bishops is being debated and decided. Some of the issues would benefit from deeper and fuller treatment than has been possible in the main chapters of a short book. We have therefore included three appendices which take the arguments further. In *Appendix One* we have reproduced Dr Michael J Ovey's substantial submission to the Rochester Commission. In this submission Dr Ovey explores in depth the theological context of the consecration of women bishops, the exegesis of relevant texts within than context, and some of the arguments pertaining to justice and Reception – all within the framework of 'the economy of salvation'.

In *Appendix Two* – much shorter – we have reproduced the text of Professor Anthony Thiselton's speech to the General Synod in July 2010. In that speech Professor Thiselton analysed St Paul's understanding of collaborative ministry in the context of his own oversight of churches – one in which he does not exalt his own status or his authority over fellow leaders.

In *Appendix Three* we have provided a note by Dr Vinay Samuel on equality and collaboration in leadership. Drawing on Biblical and philosophical material Dr Samuel argues that in the context of the women bishops debate the key issue is not how to delegate power but rather that on mutual equality in servant leadership.

Is there a better way?

It is the conviction of those who have sponsored this book that, whether one is in favour of the consecration of women bishops or against it, there must be a better way of doing this than the present Draft Measure. That conviction does not rest on opposition to the very idea of women bishops. Rather, it rests on the recognition that the arguments of those who are opposed, and the theological traditions upon which they draw, have been and are authentically Anglican. These 'loyal Anglicans' therefore deserve to be given a secure, continuing place within the Church of England. The Church of England itself and, more importantly, its future ability to sustain and develop its pastoral and evangelistic mission to the people of our nation, would be impoverished without that secure place being offered.

That such a view is not confined to opponents of the very idea of women bishops was demonstrated when the Archbishops of Canterbury and York proposed to the General Synod certain amendments to the Draft Measure. These were accepted by the majority of Synod members, but not by a majority in the House of Clergy. They were not therefore adopted because the consent of all three houses was required by the Synod's Constitution. Had the Archbishops' amendments been accepted, the concerns of those who were reluctant to agree to the Draft Measure would have been largely met.[4] In consequence the church is offered a Draft Measure which makes only discretionary provision for those parishes and clergy who cannot in conscience accept the ministry of women bishops. We believe that there is A Better Way – one which allows the consecration of women bishops but which also makes secure provision for those who cannot in conscience accept them. That would of course take time, but it would time well spent if the outcome is a

---

[4] The Archbishops argued for a new collaborative ministry by men and women in the church, and a shared leadership. They were calling for a new "wineskin", new ways of working, so that this goal could be achieved. They drew on material from various positions, showing that mono-episcopacy is not the sole model for oversight, and giving good reasons for a more plural approach to ministry, such as is found in a number of area schemes in various dioceses.

Measure which is more fully consonant with the Church of England's doctrine, and which commands fuller support across the whole church.

Some proponents of women bishops argue that provision of that kind would not be acceptable, because it would reduce women bishops to second class bishops. That perception rests on an insistence upon 'mono-episcopacy', the convention – not derived from Scripture – that in any geographical area there should be only one bishop. This, though represented in much Church of England practice, fails to take account of the shared leadership that characterises the New Testament Church and other patterns of episcopacy, such as the London Plan,[5] evident in the present life of the Church of England.

The task of finding a way to make the secure provision required, and thus maintain the unity of the church, will rest with the House of Bishops as it prepares to present the final legislation to the General Synod, probably in July 2012. Meanwhile, the legislation is being discussed in deanery and diocesan synods. We offer this symposium to members of those synods, and to the wider church, to show that there is considerable substance to the theological and ecclesiological arguments put forward by those who cannot accept the ministry of women bishops. Those arguments cannot and should not be set aside.

We are very grateful to The Latimer Trust for publishing this book which, it is hoped, will make a significant contribution to the future of the Church of England's Mission and Ministry.

PHILIP GIDDINGS

READING, OCTOBER 2011

---

[5] Under the London Plan, the Bishop of Fulham provides pastoral care for Anglo-Catholic parishes across the diocese.

1.   Kingdom and Church – equality and authority

Summary

Those who advocate a change in the Church of England's traditional order of ministry, by men and women, appeal primarily to Kingdom order; they believe that the expression of equality in contemporary society is an expression of the Kingdom of God. But the New Testament teaching on the Church, the Body of Christ, views the Church as existing not only in history but also beyond it, in heaven. We should not attempt to collapse the Church of God into the Kingdom of God.

In heaven, where God's Kingdom will be finally established, there will be no need for order, in the Church or in the family, but there is a need for order now, in this life. The phrase '[in Christ] there is neither male nor female' (Galatians 3:28, ESV) is often applied to issues of human order in the Church, in the pre-parousia world, as an argument in favour of having women priests and bishops. But this is to misapply Scripture. The context of this phrase shows that the topic being discussed is not the ordering of the Church, but the acceptance by God of all who turn to Christ in repentance and faith. The institution of marriage, however, reflects a correct understanding; marriage is rooted in the creation order, and the reality of the Kingdom of God does not set aside the creation order.

Asymmetrical equality describes the relationship of persons who are equal in their being but are in differentiated relationships of authority and function. This asymmetrical equality, which is expressed in the creation of the family, is not set aside in the relationships of the Kingdom. And it does not undermine the biblical teaching on equality in other areas of life. Family and Church reflect an asymmetrical understanding of equality that deals with questions of power, direction and nurture, in a model of relationships that reflects the Trinity. This is not diversity that makes everything in all respects equal, but a plurality that recognizes different roles.

There is a distinction between the authority of direction and the authority of domination. In the family, the authority of the male is the authority of direction, not of power. This is mirrored in the Church, in the giving to the male of the apostolic responsibility for directing what is to be taught. The Orders of the Church, which authorize people for specific authority and functions of ministry, provide for women to teach what has been agreed. This is not patriarchy, in which the source of authority and legitimation of identity and being for everyone comes from the authoritative male father, but a conformity to the order of the Trinity and of the creation.

Why is the relationship between the Church of God and the Kingdom of God so critical in the women bishops debate?

Church and culture

We believe that the Church of God addresses culture and expresses itself in cultural forms. The Kingdom of God also transforms culture. The issue of the equality of women is not just a theological issue; it also has profound cultural implications because of women's roles in society. The Anglican church has always lived out its faith and its church life in the surrounding culture. It takes culture very seriously. Therefore, the issue about the ordination of women to the episcopate is about whether the Church of England is still able to reflect and engage with the social order.

For Anglicans there is an integral relationship between church and social order, which shapes the church and gives it a moral conscience. This is an Anglican view of life and theology. The social order, however, has now changed. The church is seen as wedded to a discarded social order, giving the impression of being unable to disentangle itself from these outdated orders. The claim is made that the Kingdom of God is always moving on, and that the Church of England has refused to change.

Those who advocate a change in the church's traditional order of ministry, by men and women, appeal primarily to Kingdom order; they believe that the expression of equality in contemporary society is an expression of the Kingdom of God.

Kingdom and Church

So the relationship between the Church of God and the Kingdom of God becomes critically important for the construction of these arguments. The arguments for the equality of women in the episcopate are drawn from a Kingdom vision rather than a vision of the Church.

What is the relationship between the Church of God and the Kingdom of God?

In summary, the New Testament describes the Church as the community of God's people, the family of God. It is a love-shaped community, a faith-confessing community, a rule-based community and a mission-driven community.

The Church in and beyond history

In the teaching of Jesus, the Kingdom of God is both a present reality and a future hope. Jesus' teaching about the Kingdom of God has been recovered within the institution of the church and, in particular, within the evangelical movement in the past fifty years. This has led, in some instances, to the Church of God on earth being seen as provisional, in contrast to the eternal nature of the Kingdom of God. For example, Karl Rahner wrote that 'the church is living always on the proclamation of our own provisional status and her historically advancing elimination in the coming kingdom of God towards which she is expectantly traveling as a pilgrim'.[1] Also, Hans Kung sees the Church as finite and of the present, and the Kingdom as of the future and the end time. For him and those who see the Church as existing for the Kingdom, until the Kingdom's consummation, *Ecclesia* is the work of man and *Basileia* is the work of God.[2]

Much of contemporary evangelicalism has embraced this Kingdom understanding and, as a result, suffers from an ecclesial deficit. As mission-shaped communities, evangelicals understandably draw on the Kingdom framework. They see the Church, essentially, as the agency that witnesses to the Kingdom. In his excellent paper, 'The Kingdom Master Plan: The Ecclesia',[3] Bambang Budianto appears to recover the significance of the Church. But he defines it in Kingdom language and terms that suggest the Church's provisional and temporary status, until its dissolution in the Kingdom.

---

[1] 'The Church and the Parousia of Christ', in *Theological Investigations*, vol. 6, (Helicon, Baltimore, 1969), p. 298, quoted by A. C. Dulles in *Models of the Church*, (Random House, New York, 1978), p. 95.

[2] Hans Kung, *The Church*, (Sheed and Ward, New York, 1968), pp. 92-3, quoted in Dulles, loc.cit.

[3] Unpublished paper presented at a Consultation of the International Fellowship of Evangelical Mission Theologians, Oxford, March 2010.

However, the New Testament teaching on the Church, while showing an integral relationship between the Kingdom and the Church, views the Church as existing not only in history but also beyond history, in heaven.

Avery Dulles, in *Models of the Church*, quotes the Swedish biblical scholar, Harald Riesenfeld, to affirm that the term *Ecclesia* is an eschatological term:

> The idea of the "People of the Saints of the most high God", upon whom, according to Daniel 7:27, power and glory are to be restored, lies at root of the thinking of Paul, the Synoptics and presumably even Jesus concerning the church.[4]

In 1 Corinthians 6:1-3, Christians share in God's judgment, even over the angels. Jesus taught that the little flock of his disciples, the *proto ecclesia*, would share in the messianic supper in heaven and sit on thrones. Jesus prepares a place for his disciples in his Father's house in heaven. For Paul the Church is a temple under construction that will be completed and consecrated at the end of history (Ephesians 2:22); the Church is also a bride, perfected and presented in heaven (2 Corinthians 11:2; Ephesians 5:25-27; Revelation 19:7; 21: 2; 22:17).

While the kingdoms of the world will become the Kingdom of our Lord and King at Christ's return, the Church that is the bride of Christ, the New Jerusalem, the holy temple, will also reign with him.

So we cannot collapse the Church of God into the Kingdom of God. The Church has an eternal existence. And it is this Church that we are part of, on earth and in history.

Kingdom order and order in the Church

If the Kingdom of God has to do with God's order, or rule, being witnessed to and established on earth, what is the relationship between that Kingdom order and order in the Church? Does the Church embody the Kingdom, and therefore express the realities of the New Creation in the world, now? Or is the Church just a sign? Is the Church distinct from the Kingdom – pointing to it and witnessing to it rather than expressing it? Is the implication of our message that the Church is only a sign, but is never the New Creation itself?

---

[4] Ibid., p. 96 .

The Church reflects the reality of the Kingdom in history, in the lives of its members, as a community in the world, and through the way it orders its life in the world. The Kingdom is beyond the Church. Its boundaries are not co-terminous with the Church. Yet, the Church has a distinct existence within the reality of the Kingdom, and has a particular place and life, both in history and in an eschatological future.

The Holy Spirit, who is the eschatological gift of the new age following the resurrection of Christ, is particularly poured on the Church; and the Spirit's gifts for the Church are unique, not available beyond the Church.

The Church orders its life as a divine institution in human society. It is the body of Christ in institutional form. Its members have certain callings, and gifts that go with those callings. Its relationships reflect equality, mutual submission and support. It has defined functions and orders, and codes of behaviour and discipline. All these are part of its faith, life and order, and they characterize its life.

In the biblical teaching on the Kingdom of God, however, there is very little that lays out and authorizes this order. Teaching on Kingdom ethics and values tends to displace mention of the distinct calling of the Church, which is to follow the pattern given to it as the Body of Christ and the People of God.

The Above and Below nature of the Kingdom

The above and below nature of the Kingdom is evident in the Lord's Prayer: '... your kingdom come, your will be done, on Earth as in Heaven ...'. The Kingdom is not a future reality, only for heaven. It operates in its fullness in heaven now. Its operation in history is to draw history to its fulfillment. It is real and not an imperfect kingdom. On earth it is anticipatory and not complete. On earth it is provisional, as to our understanding of it and even our expression of it, for we see in a mirror shadowed by history. But even its provisional expression strives and strains for its perfect fulfillment.

The Church, meanwhile, is endowed with the Holy Spirit and the deposit of the faith given to the Apostles; it also has the Holy Scriptures, the norm by which it lives, as the source of the truth that leads to salvation and transformation.

The Church recognizes its incompleteness and sin, and groans for heaven. Yet it is called to witness to truth that is not provisional. It is called to live confidently in the truth which, if not complete, is certainly adequate. It is called to bear witness to the truth boldly in the world. Though conscious of its frailty and sinfulness, the Church is still called, in history, to live confidently according to the truth it has been given.

The Church and the New Creation

The Church's life on earth makes it a sign of the Kingdom of God and of the New Creation. And its life as the sign is empowered by the love that the Holy Spirit pours into it. This love will enable it to develop a mode of conduct and character that conforms to God's moral law. God's moral law must shape the Church's life as much as God's love.

The Church's life on earth also makes it a space for the expression of the life of the New Creation, though its members will be deeply conscious that this life is far from its full realization. The space shaped by the love poured into the Church by the Holy Spirit is the space for the spiritual formation of its members.

In the final Kingdom, in heaven, there will be no need for order, in the Church or in the family, but there is a need for order now, in this life.

On the subject of order in the local church, a key text from Paul's epistle to the Galatians is often quoted, in support of the consecration of women as bishops: '[in Christ] there is neither male nor female' (Galatians 3:28, ESV).

There are two matters to address in connection with this text. The first is, 'When does gender cease to matter for Paul?' The second is, 'What is the relation of this statement to the creation order which Paul refers to time and again?'

To answer the first, we have to relate this to how Paul interprets this statement in his other writings for his own time. He gave differing instructions for the behaviour of men and women in the church. So he clearly did not think that, in this present order, male and female were indistinguishable or interchangeable. For Paul, gender does matter in the present age.

Further, this text has to be understood within the overall thrust of the message of Galatians, namely, how God accepts us. Acceptance by God is on the basis of faith alone. Paul makes it very clear that neither gender, nor race, nor social status can make any difference to that acceptance. None of these things can contribute to our acceptance by God. Nor can they hinder it. Acceptance is by his grace alone.

Therefore, to take Paul's teaching concerning our acceptance by God, and apply it simplistically to issues of human order in the Church in the pre-parousia world, is to misapply Scripture.

The creation order

Second, there is Paul's reference to the creation order. Paul draws on biblical teaching about the creation order because his readers were living in this creation and were not fully redeemed. In this he follows the example of Jesus. In Mark 10:6, and also its parallel in Matthew 19:4, Jesus affirms that 'from the beginning of creation, "God made them male and female" ... "and they shall become one flesh."' (ESV)

But Jesus is not imprisoned by this order. The Sadducees asked Jesus about whose wife the woman who married seven brothers would be in the resurrection, in order to show how ludicrous the concept of resurrection was. They assumed the given categories of this world, and that there would be a problem in reproducing them in a world with no death. Jesus does not address the trick question. Instead, he indicates the discontinuity between the order of this world and the order of the Resurrection, where 'they neither marry nor are given in marriage' (Matthew 22:30, ESV). It is interesting that, in this instance, Jesus does not run the argument backwards, in order to draw conclusions contrary to the creation teaching for life on earth.

He does not shy away from upholding the creation order when addressing the position of children (Matthew 18:2-5). He makes it clear that in the Kingdom order the greatest is the least, and he puts a child next to him. He makes it clear that he expects the disciples to reproduce this in the order of the Kingdom in this world: they are to receive the Kingdom as a child; the least is the greatest. His teaching confronts the practice of his time, by which a child was totally subordinate to his elders. By contrast, he makes acceptance of the child a sign of acceptance by God. If you receive a child in Jesus' name, you receive Jesus.

The traditional role and status of children is overturned because the Kingdom, as a different reality, has arrived. If Jesus could overturn the place of children in his culture, why does he not overturn the place of women in relation to men in marriage?

Jesus is willing to overturn what was merely a cultural custom (the place of children), and is able to see even the created order (of marriage) transformed in the Resurrection. Nevertheless, in the pre-*parousia* world the created order cannot be set aside. Jesus does not set it aside. So, in the institution of marriage, which is rooted in the creation order, the reality of the Kingdom does not set aside the created order. The creation order is privileged in interpreting the reality of the Kingdom.

The orders of creation

The orders of creation refer to the God-ordained arrangements for relationships within the creation, such as the relationships in a family, between the rulers of creation and the rest of creation, between the rulers and the ruled, between the state and the people. The orders of creation cannot be correctly identified by human investigation, but need to be discovered in the teaching of scripture. Human and material sciences cannot, on their own, define these orders. Grace does not add to what human intellect deduces from nature.

If the revelation found in Scripture identifies the orders of creation, it is possible that this understanding will be dominated by the cultural and contextual values of the person interpreting the revealed text. The corrective is to be found in Scripture itself and also in the community of the faithful, the Church.

The creation order is fulfilled in the Kingdom. Kingdom order does not displace the orders of creation, New Creation, Church and Kingdom. At the present time, however, people are making decisions and choices, as they read what the Kingdom and the New Creation are about. They are suggesting that the traditional teaching on the nature of the relationship between men and women does not reflect the biblical pattern and teaching.

The reason for affirming the creation order is that it is complete. It had been dismantled at the Fall. It now has to be restored, rather than completed. Eschatology is the fulfillment of what creation was always meant to be. Church and Kingdom are not historical projects that slowly develop ideas in history. So the book of Genesis is not a piece of pre-history. It is an expression of God's purpose for how relationships in the family are to be ordered, and how ministry in the Church is to be exercised.

Creation should not be viewed as being unfinished, needing to be completed in the course of history. But those who take a symmetrical (interchangeable) approach to equality suggest that the creation is unfinished and that the pattern established in creation was a mistake, which now needs correction.

The Resurrection operates in history and as an order. Creation began with an order. The Fall distorts that order. The Resurrection restores the order and enables us to participate in that order.

Understanding equality in the ordering of creation

Asymmetrical (non-interchangeable) equality in creation is not abrogated in Kingdom order, it continues. But it does not undermine the biblical teaching of equality in other areas of life. The biblical teaching on equality is not monochrome. The areas of the family and of the Church are marked out to reflect an asymmetrical understanding of equality, which deals with questions of power, direction and nurture, but not in a democratic or patriarchal fashion.

Neither democracy nor patriarchy is privileged in Scripture; instead we are given a model of relationships that reflects the Trinity. In this, the three persons of the Trinity have perfect equality of being. Their equality exists alongside the differentiation in authority and function, where the Son acknowledges the Father's authority and is obedient to the Father (John 8:28, 29), but the Father is not said to be obedient to the Son.

The relationships that we are to seek in the Christian family, ordained by God for our good, are the relationships that we should seek for all families. And here we need to focus on the nature of equality.

The ordering of relationships has to do with connections. In creation the ordering is both vertical and horizontal, and the connections are both hierarchical and horizontal.

Hierarchical connections are the connections between the creation and the Creator. They are also between the animal and plant world, on the one hand, and humanity, charged by the Creator with the stewardship of creation, on the other.

These connections set out the direction and purpose for each order. Men and women are to steward the animal and plant world which, in the pre-Fall situation, is to co-operate with humanity. And men and women are to do this in obedience to the Creator.

The relationships, or connections, have two aspects: the aspect of the overseer and carer, for one party, and the aspect of reciprocating, nurturing and mutual love, for the other party. This is what we see in the relationship between humanity and the animal and plant world: the man and the woman were to work and care for the Garden of Eden, and the garden was to provide food for the man and woman.

This is not a diversity that makes everything equal, in all aspects; it is a plurality that recognizes different roles.

The role of humanity, as God commands in Genesis 1:28, is to 'Be fruitful and increase in number; fill the earth and subdue it. Rule over the fish of the sea and the birds of the air and over every living creature that moves on the ground.' (NIV). This rule is not mastery or domination, but the rule of stewardship, of care. The animal and plant world is directed by men and women, but it does not praise or worship them. It praises and worships God.

Men and women are there as stewards who obey God, recognizing that it is God who has put creation under their care. Psalm 8:6 acknowledges this: 'You made him ruler over the works of your hands; you put everything under his feet: all flocks and herds, and the beasts of the field, the birds of the air, and the fish of the sea, all that swim the paths of the seas.' (NIV). As creatures themselves, and not sovereign rulers, men and women are to serve God in obedience, caring for the earth and its creatures, and directing it according to God's will and purpose.

Direction not domination

What is the nature of the authority that is being exercised here? In the Old Testament there are two types of authority, didactic authority, which means directing, and political authority, which means power and domination, the power of a master over a slave, one person deciding on behalf of another. And Old Testament teaching makes it clear that, in the family, the authority of the male is the authority of directing, not of power.

As the Church of England continues to support and encourage women to teach in the church, and recognizes their teaching role by ordination to the diaconate and the presbyterate, it would be proper to assert that the apostolic role of deciding what is to be taught is to be reserved for the male. When confronted by people who were neither commissioned by them, nor attached to them, neither Jesus nor Paul prevented people from teaching in their name. Their focus was on what was taught, rather than the sanctioned status of those who were teaching. Their concern was for the truth. For Paul, the truth was preserved through the apostolic order of the male apostle and male head of the family.

When these two roles, the role of directing and the role of power, are confused in marriage, the result is oppression. Recently (April 2011), we were reminded of the truth of this by the Bishop of London, Bishop Richard Chartres, who quoted the English poet, Chaucer, in the course of his sermon at the Royal Wedding of Prince William and Kate Middleton. He said:

> Marriage should transform, as husband and wife make one another their work of art. This transformation is possible as long as we do not harbour ambitions to reform our partner. There must be no coercion if the Spirit is to flow; each must give the other space and freedom. Chaucer, the London poet, sums it up in a pithy phrase:
>
> 'Whan maistrie [mastery] comth, the God of Love anon, Beteth his wynges, and farewell, he is gon.'

If, in a marriage, the male does not take his place under God, obeying God in his directing role, then disfunction sets in. Fights happen when the political is confused with the directional, and when the woman becomes totally dependent on the man.

If, however, asymmetrical equality is the relationship that God intends for men and women in marriage, in the human family, it ought to be so in the family of the local church as well (see 1 Timothy 3:5 and 1 Timothy 5:1-2).

Patriarchy, equality and power

Gender can be expressed in patriarchy. In patriarchy, everything comes through the male father who is the fount of everything and the gatekeeper. All power is held from one central source. Male headship in Scripture does not affirm patriarchy and is not the same as patriarchy.

Patriarchy is ruling over others. In the Genesis narrative this is said to be the consequence, after the Fall, for unredeemed humanity; it is not the purpose of creation. The words are not prescriptive, but descriptive; the responsibility of being the head becomes a curse, and the male becomes the domineering tyrant.

In the book of the prophet Joel we read that the Holy Spirit will come on 'sons and daughters' and 'young men' (Joel 2:28, NIV). This undermines any notion that all spiritual and religious life must come through the male father. And the prophet Jeremiah speaks of the law of God being written on people's hearts (Jeremiah 31:33), as opposed to being transmitted through the male father. But now, in the women bishops debate, the word 'patriarchy' is used to describe and to undermine all forms of Scriptural male headship. This is false. There is even a description, in Proverbs 31, of an economically independent wife. This woman is both a member of the family and an economically independent business woman, and her description is a direct challenge to the idea that the Bible promotes patriarchy.

The biblical ideal for men and women is that each person should be desired for himself or herself. See the Song of Songs for confirmation of this. Woman is not defined as a childbearer, she is a companion, to be desired for herself. As for male headship, ideally this will reflect the headship of Christ, who is not a patriarch but the head of the Church, his bride, whom he serves.

Obedience does not mean deference and subordination. The pattern we should follow is the submission, in the Trinity, of God the Son to God the Father. In the Trinity there is equality, but it is an asymmetrical equality since the different persons of the Trinity have different roles.

Conclusion

The above argument confirms the Church's commitment to maintaining the creation order in the Church until the *parousia*. We do not have the fullest expression of the nature of the perfected Church in heaven, so we cannot speculate on that. The Church has made no distinction between the roles of male and female saints, so there is an argument that this asymmetry is not eternal. But this is no reason for overthrowing the orders set for creation.

These orders obtain in both the family and the Church because these are the settings in which new life is brought into being and nurtured.

2. False Premises and Failed Promises

Summary

In this chapter we set out the case that, by consecrating women as bishops, the Church of England will have decisively endorsed an understanding of human identity which is fundamentally at odds with that of Scripture. This is not to argue that all who support the innovation are ideological feminists, but that, despite appearances, there is ultimately no middle ground. Mary Wollstonecraft is widely recognized as a seminal figure for the feminist movement, but her utopian and secular rationalism, with its debt to the ideals of the French Revolution, stands in clear contrast to the biblical and moral radicalism of her late-eighteenth-century contemporary, William Wilberforce. Claims that the consecration of women as bishops is a form of obedience to the Holy Spirit need, therefore, to be scrutinized very carefully, not only because of the implicit claim that the Holy Spirit seems to have allowed the Church to continue in a fundamental error for many centuries, but also because it would be naïve in the extreme not to consider the possibility that we may have a form of ideological entryism on our hands.

That this is indeed the case is strongly suggested by the way in which proponents of female bishops have been ready to abandon the accommodation of the 'two integrities', established by the 1993 Act of Synod. The forcing of conscience that this will entail parallels the use of the language of rights, in order to force Christian conscience in wider society, and this at a time when understandings of gender, complementarity and mutuality, rooted in the Judaeo-Christian tradition, are being eroded. At stake here, we believe, is the biblical understanding of human identity, of which gender is an essential, and not an accidental, part, and also the understanding of human freedom as flowing from mutuality rather than the struggle for autonomy.

Beliefs do, of course, have consequences, and we note how the outworking of feminist commitments, as part of a massive social experiment over the past fifty years, has fallen far short of the hopes that its advocates held out. Yet this does not seem to have inhibited the

Church of England from an uncritical endorsement of feminism in the most iconic way possible.

Discerning the Spirit

Christina Rees, a leading advocate for women as bishops and until recently chair of the pressure group WATCH (Women and the Church), has recently made the bold claim that she is ...

> ... not following the spirit of the age, but the Spirit in the age, and what I mean by that is the divine spirit that is telling me and thousands of others that this basic inequality of the sexes is wrong and has been for so many centuries ...[1]

This is a remarkable statement, not only insofar as 'the Spirit *in* the age' and 'the spirit *of* the age' seem to be saying the same thing, but also in its implication that the Holy Spirit has allowed the Church to labour under a mistaken understanding of Holy Orders for some two millennia. According to Jesus, the Spirit is 'the Spirit of truth, whom the world cannot receive, because it neither sees him nor knows him' (John 14:17, ESV). So, if what is claimed to be the leading of the Spirit happens to coincide with a current cultural movement – in this case a feminist-inspired understanding of gender equality – it is especially important to assure ourselves that the truth being claimed is harmonious with revealed truth, as we have it through the Spirit-inspired Scriptures and as illuminated by apostolic tradition.

Our conviction is that this claim of divine sanction for consecrating women as bishops is not only biblically unsustainable, but also that it gives powerful endorsement to a form of feminism which has disastrously weakened the family and the traditional Judaeo-Christian structures of society. Just at the time when the evidence of social breakdown is becoming irresistible,[2] the Church of England

---

[1] Interview at http://wrinkledweasel.blogspot.com/p/wavelengths-3.html. Accessed 26th May 2011.

[2] For two recent examples see:

1) 'Why is the Government anti-Marriage? Family Policy derived from strong evidence would lead to policies which supported Marriage' by the Centre for Social Justice, December 2009 http://www.centreforsocialjustice.org.uk/client/downloads/Marriage%20Paper%20FINAL%20_ii_.pdf Accessed 26th May 2011.

2) 'The Good Childhood Report' by The Children's Society, February 2009 www.childrenssociety.org.uk Accessed 26th May 2011.

seems determined to press ahead and entrench an historic change to its understanding of Holy Orders, embedding the assumptions of a cultural experiment which is clearly failing.

We are not, of course, suggesting that all those who are in favour of women bishops are ideological feminists, but we do want to point out that, in this debate, there is finally no middle ground. We are concerned that those who are persuaded by the case for women bishops should be fully aware of the extent to which feminist assumptions, about gender interchangeability and the patriarchal nature of the family and marriage, inform this innovation and could be reinforced by it.

At the heart of the case for admitting women to the presbyterate, and now to the episcopate, is an appeal to fairness, lest the Church of England lag behind wider society. It relies on the language of discrimination, and invites a precise equivalence with discrimination on grounds of race. Those who wish to maintain the traditional and, as they would see it, biblical, patterns of ministry are therefore presented with a simple choice – to discriminate or not. And if they do wish to discriminate, the onus is on them to produce arguments sufficiently strong to overturn what is presented as a basic human right. They are therefore immediately put on the back foot, required to defend what in the eyes of many is the indefensible.

But this way of framing the question needs to be challenged. Discrimination in itself is morally neutral. It becomes wrong when it is, to put it most simply, unfair – when it is arbitrary and causes harm to those discriminated against. In this chapter we shall question the feminist 'fairness' argument by questioning two of its premises from a biblical perspective: firstly, to do with identity – the *naturalist* assumption that gender is *inessential* to human identity, just a matter of biological difference, and secondly, to do with autonomy – the *rationalist* assumption that personal autonomy is *essential* to fully human identity.

Sex and the soul

Although the prospect of women in the episcopate appears to be a novelty, the assumptions which energise the advocates of this claimed right can be traced back to the late eighteenth century. In the spirit of the French Revolution, Mary Wollstonecraft wrote *A Vindication of the Rights of Woman* (1792) which laid the foundations of modern feminist thought. As a rationalist (but not an atheist), she grounded the equality of men and women in reason; the only defensible basis of obedience to authority was not tradition but reason. And she believed that human flourishing would only come about when the inequalities represented by traditional authority structures, such as the Monarchy, the Church and the Army, had been removed.

Although she imagines an idealised picture of family life, she is so preoccupied with what she saw as the widespread dysfunctionality of the family that a deep suspicion of marriage pervades her thought. Women needed to be emancipated from their subjection to men through traditional authority structures, in which marriage played a key part. Much of what passed for feminine qualities in late-eighteenth-century society, especially the cultivation of aesthetic sensibilities, she saw as a form of arrested development, arising from this male oppression. Her preoccupation with equality led her argue that gender was no longer constitutive of human identity. Instead, gender boils down to an essentially biological difference, and she writes,

> But if it be not philosophical to think of sex when the soul is mentioned, the inferiority must depend on the organs; or the heavenly fire, which is to ferment the clay, is not given in equal portions.[3]

It may certainly be conceded that Wollstonecraft's critique of the place of women in the society of her time was far from groundless, but her project goes well beyond reform; its underlying assumptions were also those which informed the French Revolution. In the political sphere that particular strand of Enlightenment thinking which took shape as Communism in its Marxist-Leninist form was finally discredited with the fall of the Iron Curtain; its underlying utopianism, however, had already been powerfully critiqued by political philosophers, perhaps most notably by Sir Isaiah Berlin, as will be discussed below. However, the critique of ideas derived from Enlightenment rationalism within the *cultural* sphere has not, so far, been as effective. Although there are many varieties of feminist critique today, the movement is still very much a product of Enlightenment assumptions, in so far as it is taken as axiomatic that men oppress women through patriarchal social structures, of which the traditional family is the foundation. Yet the results of this experiment have not been encouraging, as we shall argue,

---

[3] A *Vindication of the Rights of Woman*, (Cosimo Classics, New York, 2008), p.30.

and they suggest that the presuppositions of feminism need to be evaluated critically against the biblical narrative.

The conservative response to the radical ideas of the Enlightenment was articulated most comprehensively by Edmund Burke, in his *Reflections on the Revolution in France* (he and Wollstonecraft both died in 1797). He rightly identified a utopian confidence in reason as the essential and dangerous flaw in the revolutionary movement. But the unfortunate legacy of that necessary protest was that it helped to entrench a concept of Christianity as an essentially reactionary and backward-looking guarantor of social order. The development of liberation and feminist theologies on the liberal wing of the Church is too often simply the other side of the coin – a dysfunctional reaction to an existing dysfunction just makes the dysfunctionality worse.

Radically different radicals

The very idea of living under any kind of traditional and, especially, religious authority is, of course, deeply alien to feminism and to postmodern Western intellectuals in general. But the French Revolution took place in a country which had not experienced a Reformation; in an English context, even with an Established Church, it was not so clear that Christianity was invariably the agent of an inflexible status quo. One of the best and most well-known examples of the transformational potential of biblical Christianity is the long campaign of William Wilberforce against the slave trade. Unlike Mary Wollstonecraft, his contemporary (they were both born in 1759), the emancipation he sought was not inspired by the utopianism of the French Revolution, attempts by his opponents to tar him with the same revolutionary brush notwithstanding. Instead, he was sustained by the biblical convictions of his evangelical Christian faith, as he persevered for some twenty years against the grain of British economic interests. As Niall Ferguson comments,

> It is not easy to explain so profound a change in the ethics of a people. It used to be argued that slavery was abolished simply because it had ceased to be profitable, but all the evidence points the other way: in fact, it was abolished despite the fact that it was

still profitable.[4]

The brand of feminism which appeared in the 1960s, and which has energised the campaign for women's ordination, has a much more ambiguous relationship to market forces, as will be explored below.

Wilberforce's radicalism was very far from that of the French Revolution; he believed that the transformation of British society would come about only through changing the moral behaviour of individuals, not through political revolution. So this biblical radicalism entailed a degree of conservatism; his opposition to the French Revolution and its sympathisers in England was not simply a matter of political expediency, but also a principled conservatism which recoiled from the anti-Christian polemic of the revolutionaries and their utopian deification of human reason.

Such recognition of man's imperfectability is consistent with the Anglican Reformers' awareness of human fallibility; even those entrusted with the leadership of the Church were seen as fallible. The Thirty-nine Articles acknowledge this truth, to the extent of acknowledging that General Councils of the Church may not be reliable, '(forasmuch as they be an assembly of men, whereof all be not governed with the Spirit and Word of God,) they may err' (Article XXI). If this is the case, how much more should we hesitate before 'baptising' social and political movements, whether of the Left or the Right, as being expressions of the Kingdom?[5] This conservatism is not about being backward-looking, but a biblical awareness that the truly transformational power of the gospel will be compromised if it is subsumed to the passing political and cultural enthusiasms of the day. For sure we have a foretaste of the Kingdom to come, in the incarnation and in the presence of the outpoured Spirit of God, but the attempt to build 'Kingdom' structures or movements is in essence to repeat the error of St Peter on the Mount of Transfiguration, to be activists who try to perpetuate divine initiative by human ingenuity. The answer now is

---

[4] Niall Ferguson, *Empire: How Britain Made The Modern World*, (Penguin, London, 2004).

[5] This possibility of error could also have radical consequences, as it did at the Reformation, in justifying the abrogation of traditions held to be contrary to Scripture. But Cranmer and the sixteenth-century Reformers were deeply versed in the Church Fathers, and this patristic 'ballast' served to keep their elevation of the authority of Scripture from becoming a pretext for anarchy.

essentially the same as then – 'Listen to him' – a principle we honour by listening attentively to Scripture.

Whatever the superficial similarities in their concern for emancipation, it is clear that Wilberforce and Wollstonecraft represent two very different understandings of human rights and freedom. It is also clear that the movement for women's ordination has proved to owe more to the latter than the former. Surely only those convinced by the language of secular rights could be sufficiently confident to overturn the accepted and centuries-old order of the Church? The legislation for women bishops in its current form displays a startling lack of regard and sense of mutuality towards others within the Church, who believe their consciences to be governed by biblical authority and ancient practice. But this is the manifestation, in the Church, of a familiar problem which has long been recognized by political philosophers.

True freedom

For modern Western societies, authority is deeply problematic because of the Enlightenment inheritance which promotes the autonomy of the individual. In its more libertarian form, this becomes the imperative to enjoy a negative freedom, 'freedom from' to use Sir Isaiah Berlin's phrase, and tends to degenerate into a solvent of a common morality and social virtue. In its more utopian and ideological form, the autonomy of the individual is subsumed into that of the state or the collective, described by Berlin as 'positive freedom'. His particular concern was that the Enlightenment's rejection of religiously grounded authoritarianism opened the way to a new authoritarianism. Once a group of decision-makers achieve power and have decided what is rational, the way is open for what Berlin has called 'the rule of experts'; these experts have the right to require individual citizens to comply with the rule of reason, even if that rule is not evidently reasonable to the individual.

Although expressed classically in the Marxist dictatorship of the proletariat, it would be a mistake to think that ideological compulsion is now a thing of the past. With the decline of Judaeo-Christian values in Western societies, a new form of totalitarianism is appearing with its own vision of positive freedom. As Melanie Phillips comments,

> A set of false assumptions about the family, men and sexual identity has become embedded in political and cultural discourse to such an extent that its distortions and evasions are

not only unrecognized but to point them out invites derision and disbelief..... It is the gender equivalent of Stalinism's big lie.[6]

In this situation it is easy for established rights to be considered obsolete if they do not command majority support – or at least the support of a parliamentary majority, which is not necessarily the same thing. Politically, we see this tendency in debates on legislation to do with abortion, marriage, homosexuality, euthanasia and freedom of speech. Ecclesiastically, it is expressed in the assumption that the Church of England's General Synod has the authority to set aside ancient Apostolic and Catholic order by majority vote, as happened in 1992 with the decision to ordain women to the presbyterate/priesthood.[7] Now the pretence of mutuality, the so-called 'two integrities', is being discarded; as it stands, the draft legislation of 2010 to allow the consecration of women to the episcopate overturns the assurances given in 1992 that the consciences of opponents would not be forced. Thus General Synod has made it clear that yesterday's majority has no authority over today's majority. Instead of acting as a brake on this majoritarianism, some senior parliamentarians make clear their desire to encourage it. Frank Field MP put down an Early Day Motion on 27th January 2011 which raised the possibility that Parliament itself would impose the legislation in its current form, if there were any attempt to amend it to accommodate those opposed on grounds of conscience. Such an interference is clearly in breach of Article XXXVII of the Thirty-nine Articles, which states that '... we give not to our Princes the ministering either of God's Word, or of the Sacraments'.

---

[6] Melanie Phillips, *The Sex Change Society*, (The Social Market Foundation, London, 1999), p.135.

[7] There has been a long-established historical awareness of the dangers of this crude majoritarianism. As Mike Ovey observes, 'The ecclesiological risks in creating a primacy of the current majority are in fact grave. They were of course adverted to in Tract 90 where Newman commented 'Religious changes, to be beneficial, should be the act of the whole body; they are worth little if they are the mere act of a majority.' Perhaps more significant is the work of John of Salisbury who noted the danger of ecclesiastical tyranny in his seminal and influential work *Policraticus*. A hallmark of tyranny in John of Salisbury's view is precisely the failure to accept one's position under law with a limited jurisdiction granted by God. To the extent that majoritarianism can create the impression of *vox populi, vox dei*, John of Salisbury would see this as ecclesiastical tyranny'. Mike Ovey, *Submission to the Rochester Commission* (6.2.15).

So how has it come about, that those who want to uphold what are described as 'traditional' values and practices find themselves on the defensive, and that the obvious injustice being perpetrated against them is ignored by those in Parliament, who ought to be protecting the Church? Here it is helpful to note that there is an asymmetry between 'negative' and 'positive' freedoms. 'Freedom from' is attractive when there is some clear and strongly felt limitation to freedom, but it is essentially negative; it does not give a sense of purpose beyond the removal of the constraint. In contrast, 'freedom for' embodies a continuing purpose to which the autonomy of the individual may be subordinated.

The way in which the campaign for women's admission to the episcopate is being conducted strongly suggests more than the removal of a constraint. It has not been enough to remove the obstacles to female ordination – this must now be established as a norm to which everyone must acquiesce. It is therefore not surprising that there has been a marked reluctance to consider the question of whether or not the monarchical form of episcopacy, into which women wish to be consecrated, is the only model which can claim support in Scripture and tradition.[8] If the critique of mono-episcopacy set out in Appendices 2 and 3 below were to be taken seriously, this would allow for overlapping jurisdictions, thereby preserving the pattern of 'two integrities' as established by the Act of Synod of 1993.

This ecclesiastical feminism is looking more and more like a typical form of ideological egalitarianism – it is conducted on the basis of claimed rights and is now sweeping aside established norms and prior commitments on the authority of voting majorities. This is the very criticism that Edmund Burke made of the massive social experiment of the French Revolution, as its tragic consequences unfolded:

> Of this I am certain, that in a democracy, the majority of the citizens is capable of exercising the most cruel oppressions upon the minority whenever strong divisions prevail in that kind of polity.[9]

---

[8] Even on feminist grounds, it might be thought that the advocates of women bishops would also want to examine carefully a model of episcopacy which has been shaped exclusively by men, and which must surely be seen as having been a key institutional expression of patriarchy.

[9] Edmund Burke, *Reflections on the Revolution in France*, (OUP, Oxford, 1999), p.126.

From the perspective of biblically-based reform developed above, which transcends Left and Right, pragmatic conservatism and ideological utopianism, it has to be said that the proponents of women bishops appear to have espoused the wrong sort of positive freedom. They are right to recognize that freedom needs to be purposeful, but they have adopted a degraded form of freedom, a human idealism which is a poor substitute for that hope which the Apostle Paul describes as 'the glorious liberty of the children of God' (Romans 8:21, KJV).

The economy of God

The Church anticipates this liberty, albeit imperfectly, insofar as the paradox of freedom and authority is resolved in Church leadership, which is itself submitted to the rule of the God who is Trinity. As Mike Ovey has stated in his submission to the Rochester Commission (see Appendix 1),

> A fundamental of Trinitarian theology has been that the economic Trinity (the Trinity as it acts in the economy of creation and redemption) reveals the immanent Trinity (the Trinity as it is in eternity). This has been the historic view of the church, forcefully formulated by Tertullian (Against Praxeas), adopted by Athanasius on the basis of John 14:6-11 (Against the Arians) and recently re-articulated by K. Rahner. (3.2.12).

The point of this distinction, between the economic and the immanent, is that it shows that equality is consistent with complementarity. Each person of the Godhead is fully God, but is unique. The uniqueness is not something illusory or temporary, but eternal and intrinsic to the Godhead. As Bishop John Rodgers summarises,

> The Father is unique in being unbegotten and in eternally begetting the Son and breathing out the Spirit. The Son is unique in being eternally begotten of the Father. The Spirit is unique in being eternally generated by, or breathed out by the Father who is the fountainhead of all Divinity.[10]

This is therefore a form of equality to which complementarity is essential; human beings, male and female, are made in the image of this God, who is Trinity.

---

[10] Bishop John Rodgers, *Essential Truths*, (Classical Anglican Press. 2011), p.31.

While care needs to be taken in applying this Trinitarian model to human relationships, which are inevitably marred by sin, we can nonetheless see that it provides a unique and powerful model for the divine economy, for fruitful relationships within the Church and society as a whole, patterned on the nature of God himself. An understanding of complementarity lies at the heart of the model, and it therefore poses the question, what does the biblical revelation require of a man and a woman respectively, in terms of their service to the Church? Specifically it raises the question of what women's ministry should look like, but this is persistently ignored by the Church of England which has, instead, co-opted women into a male pattern of ordained ministry. We will see in Chapter 3 how this Trinitarian insight provides a framework for understanding the specific teaching of the New Testament about the role of women in church leadership, but here we can sketch out the basis of a richer understanding of human flourishing, male and female, than that embodied in feminism's assumptions about fairness and freedom.

Firstly, the three-in-oneness of the Trinity enables us to see that there is an understanding of equality which does not entail the rejection of authority. The Son is subject to the Father and, in the incarnation, he humbles himself to death upon the cross (Philippians 2:5-11). His subsequent exaltation is not the conferring of divinity, but the glorious manifestation of his eternal Sonship. Similarly, the Spirit is subject to the Father and the Son, yet he shares fully in the divine personhood as one who speaks, equips and teaches, and who can be quenched and grieved. Within the essential equality of the Trinity, therefore, there are *asymmetrical relationships of dependence*, and it is this Trinitarian understanding of authority which is reflected in marriage and the family. St Paul urges the husband and wife to conceive of their relationship as being like that between Christ and his bride, the Church (Ephesians 5:22-33); he does not expect Christ to be subject to his bride, the Church.[11]

In contrast, the models of equality being deployed in the argument for women bishops are not biblical, even though biblical texts are used in support. These models derive from a notion of *symmetrical*

---

[11] Notwithstanding the call to mutual submission of v21, 'the strict reciprocity construction of Ephesians 5:21 ('each other') must be adjudged a clear failure'. (Ovey, 3.2.10)

relationships of independence, based on the idea that each person is an autonomous individual, with a centre of consciousness capable of radical freedom and agency. A particular person may happen to have a female gender but no impediment should be put in her way to express agency and capacity. This concept has not been sufficiently established from the specific texts of Scripture which speak of gender and Church leadership in the context of creation,[12] as will be argued below, but it is already apparent that it embodies a concept of human identity

---

[12]   What Mary Wollstonecraft, writing in *A Vindication of the Rights of Woman*, sees as simply a contradiction, in Milton's portrayal of the relationship between Adam and Eve in *Paradise Lost*, does actually make more sense if we read Milton within a complementarian perspective. Wollstonecraft writes:

Children, I grant, should be innocent; but when the epithet is applied to men, or women, it is but a civil term for weakness. For if it be allowed that women were destined by Providence to acquire human virtues, and by the exercise of their understandings, that stability of character which is the firmest ground to rest our future hopes upon, they must be permitted to turn to the fountain of light, and not forced to shape their course by the twinkling of a mere satellite. Milton, I grant, was of a very different opinion; for he only bends to the indefeasible right of beauty, though it would be difficult to render two passages, which I now mean to contrast, consistent: but into similar inconsistencies are great men often led by their senses:—

'To whom thus Eve with perfect beauty adorned:
My author and disposer, what thou bidst
Unargued I obey; so God ordains;
God is thy law, thou mine; to know no more
Is woman's happiest knowledge and her praise.'

These are exactly the arguments that I have used to children; but I have added, "Your reason is now gaining strength, and, till it arrives at some degree of maturity, you must look up to me for advice: then you ought to THINK, and only rely on God."

Yet, in the following lines, Milton seems to coincide with me, when he makes Adam thus expostulate with his Maker:—

'Hast thou not made me here thy substitute,
And these inferior far beneath me set?
Among unequals what society
Can sort, what harmony or delight?
Which must be mutual, in proportion due
Given and received; but in disparity
The one intense, the other still remiss
Cannot well suit with either, but soon prove
Tedious alike: of fellowship I speak
Such as I seek fit to participate
All rational delight.'

fundamentally at odds with what we would expect of human beings made in the image of God, and for relationship with God.

Secondly, the Trinity shows us that freedom does not necessarily entail the rejection of authority. In other words, autonomy (which in any case is normally quite tightly circumscribed by life's circumstances) is not in itself a precondition for freedom. But this is not to open the door to the authoritarianism of so-called 'positive freedom' which so exercised Isaiah Berlin. This is a different sort of positive freedom, clearly expressed in the relationship between the Father and the Son; although the Son has the capacity to be conscious of what it would be not to obey the Father's will, and the capacity to do so (e.g. Luke 4:1-13; 22:42), he lives in obedience to the Father's authority, because only in this way is he free to fulfill the work which will be finished upon the cross. He is radically dependent upon the Father: '... the Son can do nothing of his own accord, but only what he sees the Father doing.' (John 5:19, ESV), and precisely for this reason he is radically independent – free from intimidation and manipulation. For example, in reply to the critics of his healing on a Sabbath he says, 'My Father is working until now, and I am working.' (John 5:17, ESV) This is a relationship in which radical freedom is premised upon radical submission, a profound paradox which takes men and women to the heart of the cross.

Therefore, even before specific texts are examined, we should be cautious about any argument based on the idea that, Kingdom order being equality, this should expressed in some kind of equality of opportunity in Church hierarchy. A Trinitarian order recognizes that authority within the Trinity finds its origin in the Father, and this, by analogy and illuminated by the order of creation, should predispose us to think that within the Church the exercise of authority is an essentially male role. Moreover, this understanding of authority does not overthrow equality; in Christ we are all sons and daughters of the living God, on the absolutely equal standing of grace alone, and we subject ourselves to godly authority as that which is intended to free us to fulfill a particular role in the divine purpose.

It may be objected that this Trinitarian argument proves too much; if gender is such an essential part of human identity, can this principle of male authority be limited simply to Church and family? Does it not also, and inevitably, rule out what many would see as one of the great gains of the previous century, as the abuses which had been so evident to Mary Wollstonecraft were acknowledged, and women came to play a much fuller part in political, economic and cultural life? In response, it can be said that male headship[13] in the New Testament is affirmed in the specific context of Church and family, so the question of gender equality in other spheres may be considered more open. Indeed, the Old Testament context includes a positive encouragement of female enterprise, in its celebration of the married business woman in Proverbs 31, while Deborah is a notably effective judge of Israel and Huldah a prominent prophetess.[14] However, this position leaves an unresolved question about the coherence of the biblical witness; the question remains, if male headship is rooted in the natural and supernatural (Trinitarian) order of things, why is it that we insist upon it so strongly only within the spheres of Church and family?

A clue lies in the way Thomas Cranmer expanded the Latin *familia,* family, from the Gregorian Sacramentary in his collects for the Fifth Sunday after the Epiphany and the Twenty Second Sunday after Trinity in his prayer Book of 1549. God is beseeched 'to keep thy church and household' and 'to keep thy household the church' respectively. The household is, of course, a biblical metaphor for the Church (Galatians 6:10, 1 Peter 4:17), a metaphor that is reflected in Paul's requirement that both overseers and deacons must be those who manage their households well (1 Timothy 3:5,12). The aptness of the

---

[13] The specifically Christian character of this 'headship' authority, which is to be carefully distinguished from authoritarianism, is discussed in Chapter 3 below.

[14] On the argument that as Judges, these women were comparable to New Testament presbyters, Mike Ovey helpfully observes that the New Testament draws a distinction between preaching and prophecy. This not only helps to resolve the apparent contradiction between 1 Corinthians 11:3ff and 1 Corinthians 14: 33b-36, but also 'helps explain an oft-cited conundrum, the place of Deborah and Huldah. Deborah and Huldah are both prophetesses (Judges 4:4 and 2 Kings 22:14) whose ministries fall within the scope of 1 Corinthians 11:3ff. Deborah is also described as judging Israel (Judges 4:4, 5) but it is dubious to see this as at odds with the provisions of 1 Timothy 2:11-15 or 1 Corinthians 14:33b-36, for what is at stake in these passages is the instruction of the mixed assembly of God's people and the decisive determination of the acceptability of particular material. The material in Judges tends to picture the judges as saviour figures (Judges 2:16) or those who fulfil the literal function of judges, namely determining civil disputes (see Samuel's description of his actions in 1 Samuel 12:3-5 where he depicts himself as an honest judge in the modern sense). It is then a bow drawn at a venture to equate the Old Testament judge with the New Testament pastor-teacher or presbyter. The functions are different, and the parallel therefore fails.' (Ovey, 4.1.3)

metaphor is, amongst other things, that just as the human family provides the context for natural birth and the raising of children, so the spiritual family of the Church is the context for new birth and the growth in discipleship of the children of God. Family and Church are uniquely places of birth – natural and supernatural – where there is an especial fittingness in the headship of the male as progenitor; in the natural sense in the human household, and as the one who symbolises the fatherhood of God in the household of the Church. The Latin root of the word 'authority' is *aucto* (meaning 'increase'), and this points to authority as being that which has the capacity to give life and enable. An *auctor* is the one who gives a thing its completeness, hence a *progenitor* or *founder* and, in relation to women and minors, *the guardian* (Collins Latin Dictionary).

The cunning of history

Such an understanding of family and Church was not without its faults and failings, in practice, but it was the basis for the flourishing of family life in a biblical framework of asymmetric gender relations, which had enabled a growth of freedom and a flourishing of human persons. The point where this model broke down dramatically was in the 1960s, as a new secular narrative full of apparent promise rapidly overwhelmed what had looked like a strongly Christian culture, with rising church attendances in the years after the Second World War. While the reasons for this are complex, the historian Callum Brown has produced compelling evidence to suggest that feminism was a key element in the secularising narrative. He claims that as the 1960s opened the 'immediate victim was Christianity, challenged most influentially by second-wave feminism and the recrafting of femininity'.[15] Feminism developed into a kind of cultural bulldozer, uprooting marriage and the married family, but as time passed it became clear that this sexual revolution was not going to produce new and benign social ecologies in their place. The hopes of feminist utopians, such as Germaine Greer, were disappointed. History did not take the turn it was supposed to. Instead many women found themselves isolated and purposeless, as reflected, a generation later, in Helen Fielding's phenomenally successful depiction of rootlessness and insecurity in *Bridget Jones' Diary*.

---

[15] Callum G. Brown, *The Death of Christian Britain*, (Routledge, London, 2001), p.176.

Feminism's erosion of traditional social structures has had a paradoxical consequence. For a movement associated with the Left, which would see itself as a 'progressive' force in society, the 'second-wave' feminism of the 1960s has actually demonstrated an unexpected and unintended affinity with the Right. It is often said that by the 1990s it was clear that the Right had won the economic argument and the Left had won the social argument, but for feminism it was something of pyrrhic victory. The triumph of free market capitalism, after the breakdown of the post-war Bretton Woods consensus in the West and the fall of the Iron Curtain in the East, coincided with feminism's message of empowerment and emancipation. This conveniently released women around the globe into the labour market, and exposed them to market forces in a much more direct way. The independence so prized by the feminist movement was, for many, reduced to a new subjection to the labour market. The possibility that a mother could find an independence from the market place through dependence upon a breadwinning husband was simply obliterated by feminist first principles. So, for instance, the traditional idea of a household wage disappeared, as two-earner households became the norm and the mother's role of care and nurture in family life was devalued. For well-educated women this brave new world may have been experienced as an emancipation, but for the poor and the less privileged their new found independence in the market place was more likely to be a form of waged servitude in poorly paid menial work. As one feminist writer admits,

> Disturbing as it may sound, I am suggesting that second-wave feminism has unwittingly provided a key ingredient of the new spirit of neoliberalism. Our critique of the family wage now supplies a good part of the romance that invests flexible capitalism with higher meaning and a moral point.[16]

These are realities that Christian feminists do not yet seem to have reckoned with.

The failure of feminism in its 1960s second-wave form should, instead, be leading the Church to a deeper question – how can the Church encourage and model the rebuilding of real community, which restores to marriage and the nuclear family a sense of wider belonging

---

[16] Nancy Fraser, 'Feminism, Capitalism and the Cunning of History', New Left Review 56, March-April 2009, p.97.

and purpose? The consecration of women as bishops is much more likely to hinder than to help that process.

So the question must be asked as to whether the advocates of women bishops, acting in such a way as to exclude 'traditionalists' from the Church, are so sure of their untested and untried model of persons in relationship that they can erect, on this foundation, a whole new structure, a structure that will replace the order, set out in Scripture, that has served the Church for two millennia.

The understanding of gender equality that is being deployed here is not a legitimate biblical development, and its application to the role of the episcopate is not legitimate. The fashionable suspicion of authority, and any structures that look 'patriarchal', has obscured the possibility of true freedom and creative complementarian equality in both Church and society. The fact that the one who surrendered his life for us is described as the 'Author of life' (Acts 3:15, ESV) is a powerful antidote to the idea that authority is crudely equivalent to hegemony. It is with this perspective in mind that we turn to restate equality in its biblical sense.

3. Recovering Mutuality – 'heirs together of the grace of life'

Summary

Central to the case for giving women functional equality in the Church's ordained ministry is the Apostle Paul's well known statement from Galatians 3:28, that in Christ 'there is neither male nor female', and it is commonly argued that St Paul's specific prohibitions on women exercising teaching authority are an accommodation to specific first-century contexts. However, in this chapter we develop previous material to demonstrate that this interpretation flattens out the creative interplay of gender equality and difference that we find in the New Testament.

In one of Thomas Cranmer's homilies – these were to be read in the absence of a sermon in the Book of Common Prayer services – the construction expresses this mutuality rather neatly. There are two sections of equal length: the duty of a husband to his wife, and that of a wife to her husband – the two are not simply interchangeable – and the hinge between the two sections is the beautiful description of marriage in 1 Peter 3:7, 'heirs together of the grace of life' (KJV). Marriage brings into sharp focus a more general understanding of men and women in Christ. And as we look at the specific teaching of the New Testament about women and church leadership, we seek to give proper weight to both the past and the future perspectives in Paul's thought – the extent to which his teaching on women and leadership is grounded in the order of creation, and the extent to which male and female distinctions are crucial to his eschatological understanding of the Church as the bride of Christ.

What emerges is the possibility of a rich biblical humanism of manhood and womanhood. It is inevitably strange to twenty-first century Westerners steeped in the legacy of Enlightenment rationalism, but it needs to be recovered and modelled in the Church as a corrective, both to the rather bleak quasi-androgynous reductionism to which feminism is prone, and to the narcissistic sexuality promoted by the UK's dominant celebrity culture.

Moreover, a female episcopate is not only a breach of the direct teaching of Scripture, it is also an indirect challenge to orthodox

Christology. It is not necessary to adopt a sacerdotal concept of ordained ministry to see that, by broadening the episcopate as well as the presbyterate to women, the Church invites even more strongly the assumption that it was merely a matter of cultural contingency that the flesh assumed by the Great Shepherd and the Bridegroom of the Church was male. On this basis, it then becomes possible to speculate about an 'essential' Jesus abstracted from maleness, or even to recast Christ as the female 'Christa'. In either case the door is opened to the modern forms of ancient Christological heresies which distance us from the Christ of the gospels.

Reading Scripture correctly

In the previous chapter we have noted the paradox that feminism, as a self-styled 'progressive' movement, has actually helped to loosen up the traditional family so that it could be 'demutualised', with the lives of men and women increasingly orientated to the market place as individual consumers. In this chapter, we will look at the specific teaching of the New Testament as it relates to leadership in the Church, from the standpoint of recovering a counter-cultural sense of mutuality. This, we maintain, has the capacity to be genuinely emancipatory for women and men.

In doing this, we are not overlooking a commonly-voiced objection, which claims that the Apostle Paul's teaching on Christian leadership was accommodated to the prevalent understanding of gender in his cultural context, and, that we are therefore free to find fresh expressions of Christian leadership, appropriate to our context. In drawing out the meaning of the biblical material we shall show, firstly, that Paul roots his understanding of gender relationships in the creation order, to the extent that cultural relativism on this point can only be sustained by the assumption that the whole of Scripture's teaching is an accommodation to past cultural understandings. This would be a significant departure from traditional evangelical hermeneutics. Secondly, we demonstrate that the consecration of women as bishops reinforces the trend in feminist theology towards highly problematic Christological interpretations, which decisively distance us from the historical Jesus of Nazareth. In other words, it is difficult to regard Paul's teaching as merely contextual, because it expresses a deep Christological as well as creation logic.

The episcopate, as a separate order of ministry from the presbyterate, exists only in an emergent form in the New Testament, as represented by the particular ministries of Timothy in Ephesus and Titus in Crete. So the question of whether or not the introduction of women bishops can be supported from Scripture reduces down to an argument by extension from the validity, or otherwise, of women in the presbyterate. We are therefore at risk of going over some very well-trodden ground; detailed analysis of the relevant New Testament texts is included in Appendix 1. Our approach in this chapter will be to show how the text of Scripture needs to be approached within a Scriptural framework, rather than being forced to answer questions which arise from non-Scriptural assumptions about the meaning of equality. If the question we are dealing with is thought of as a jig-saw, the preceding chapters provide a sketch of the finished picture, which helps to prevent the specific biblical texts from being forced into configurations they were never designed for.

We have already seen that the model of the Trinity alerts us to a rich understanding of equality, which does not depend upon interchangeability and uniformity. It warns us against the reductionist tendency of secular humanism to see human identity as something to be realised by the exercise of individual autonomy, to which gender is incidental and authority, alien. The Trinitarian model of being is precisely the opposite; while it defies exhaustive definition, it is not a formless mystery. The equivalence of the economic (God as he is revealed to us) and the immanent (God as is he to himself) Trinity yields an understanding of personhood in which there can be equality of nature and dignity, yet also essential difference which is expressed relationally; the Son is always the Son and the Father always the Father. The 'economy' of the Church, therefore, will be *complementarian* rather than *egalitarian*, as expressed so eloquently by one of the Apostle Paul's favourite metaphors for the Church, that of the body, in which all the diverse parts are equally indispensible and have equal concern for each other (1 Corinthians 12).

The exercise of authority

Although the proposal to include women in the episcopate has been widely acknowledged, by opponents as well as supporters, as a natural and inevitable corollary of admitting women to the presbyterate, it does bring into sharper focus the issue of authority. This is because what is distinctive about the episcopal role is the particular responsibility of the office to exercise authority, which has both passive and active aspects.

What we may term *passive authority* stems from the bishop's *symbolic* role, recognized from the earliest days in terms of being a focus of unity. In his person, the bishop acts as a personal symbol of the Church, whether it be thought of in merely functional terms, as the chief spokesman for the Church in a particular region, or in the more mystical sense of Eastern Orthodox ecclesiology, in which the bishop personifies the Church. This symbolic role entails that the bishop has a passive authority as the one who gives endorsement.

It is passive, firstly, in the sense that it flows simply from the *identity* of the bishop. The character requirements of an elder and a deacon, as laid out in 1 Timothy 3, make it absolutely clear that there can be no distinction in ordained ministry between public and private life. It is not a professional role in the modern sense, in which any law-abiding person with the requisite technical skills will do. The character of the presbyter endorses certain values for the Church and, by the same token, the gender of the presbyter endorses a particular understanding of orders, all the more so if that presbyter is the chief presbyter, the bishop. It is surely significant that Paul, writing in 1 Timothy 3 and also in Titus 1, clearly understood presbyters to be men, and this in an age when women were commonly involved in religious leadership of pagan religions and cults.

The passive authority of endorsement operates, secondly, through *institutional inertia*, as is characteristic of the Church of England and the four 'Instruments of Unity' of the Anglican Communion (the Anglican Consultative Council, the Archbishop of Canterbury, the Lambeth Conference and the Primates' Meeting). In this case silence or inaction is taken as consent. This *can* be very positive, giving people the freedom to take creative initiatives, without having to seek prior permission at every turn from the bishop. It has given rise, in many parishes, to initiatives of great energy and to creative forms of ministry. This process depends, however, upon infractions being identified and dealt with post-eventum. The system fails if infractions are ignored or dismissed. Thus the failure to take positive disciplinary action, in various parts of the Anglican Communion over recent years, has provided false teaching and immorality with tacit endorsement; it has also undermined the confidence of many Global South provinces in the Anglican Covenant process.

The *active authority* of the episcopate stems from the bishop's role as guardian of the apostolic faith. The Church cannot be left on doctrinal auto-pilot; its doctrine requires constant vigilance on the part of its leaders, lest false teachers infiltrate the flock. This is the burden of Paul's valediction to the Ephesian elders, as recorded in Acts 20, and is very much to the fore in his instructions to the 'proto-bishops', Timothy and Titus. While the instinctive modern reaction to authority is typically one of immediate suspicion, for Paul, spiritual authority in the Church is a form of service; it is also life-giving because it keeps the Church faithful to the source of its life in Christ, given through the apostolic gospel.

Keeping our heads about headship

Therefore, as we turn to the New Testament passages which bear directly on the issue of female leadership in the Church, we need to keep our heads and not be panicked by the prevailing culture. In particular, we need to bring to bear the Scriptural understanding of symbolism and authority in order to illuminate specific passages. These three texts, 1 Corinthians 11:2-16, 14:33b-36 and 1 Timothy 2:11-15, are commonly understood by advocates of female ordination to be local and limited responses to a particular cultural context, which must be controlled by the general principle of Galatians 3:28, that in Christ Jesus 'there is neither male nor female' (ESV).

However, this fails to take into account the fact that, in all three passages, Paul's understanding of the role of women is rooted in his understanding of the order of creation, as is his teaching about male headship in marriage and the family in Ephesians 5:25-33. In this passage Paul's argument *looks back* to the reality of male and female as God-given identities in creation, and he quotes Genesis 2:24: '"Therefore a man shall leave his father and mother and hold fast to his wife, and the two shall become one flesh."' (v.31, ESV). But his argument also *looks forward* to an eschatological fulfillment of this creation reality, in the 'plan for the fullness of time' (Ephesians 1:10, ESV), when the Church is presented to Christ as his bride, 'in splendour, without spot or wrinkle' (v.27, ESV). So this should be the context for understanding gender roles in the Church now: the gospel does not nullify the natural order, but redeems it as an eschatological anticipation of the new heaven and new earth, within all the contingencies, inadequacies and failings of the Church between the times.

In 1 Corinthians 11:2-16, Paul envisages the full participation of women, as part of a mixed congregation, in prayer and prophecy, but it is distinctively as women that they participate. Paul has a strong sense of how rich this diversity is – male and female finding the fullest expression of their masculinity and femininity, not in selfish autonomy but in mutual dependence upon each other and the Lord. This will be within the framework of submission to the male leadership of that mixed congregation, something that is not demeaning but actually glorious, patterned on the Trinity itself. The controlling principle for Paul is that of headship, 'the head of every man is Christ, and the head of a wife is her husband, and the head of Christ is God.' (v.3, ESV).

The meaning of the Greek word *kephale* (meaning 'head'), used by Paul in this passage and similarly in Ephesians 5:23, has, of course, been contested, but a Trinitarian pattern of mutual dependence accords with the position of Professor Anthony Thiselton, who rejects the meaning of 'source' in preference for 'head', understood not in terms of a controlling centre of power, with its undertones of patriarchy, but in a metaphorical sense. He notes that 'head' has 'unfortunate associations with domination and mastery in the modern world which fail to fit Paul's precise meaning', and adds that 'The *kephale* of a family is the one who represents its "public face", the *representative contact person* who *focuses* its identity, but it does *not absorb or assimilate* its identity.'[1]

It is therefore no more demeaning for women to assert male headship than it is demeaning for Christ to assert the headship of the Father. In fact, this acknowledgment of headship is very far from demeaning – it is the key to what is truly glorious in human existence. Here we see how the Trinitarian understanding of identity and authority helps to make sense of what might otherwise seem obscure and contradictory.

In verses 7 and 8, Paul expands on the idea of headship as being rooted in the sequence of creation; man is created first, for the glory of God, and woman is then created from man. So what are we to make of Paul's statement that 'woman is the glory of man' (v.7, ESV)? The

---

[1] Anthony C. Thiselton, *1 Corinthians: A Shorter Exegetical and Pastoral Commentary*, (Eerdmans, Grand Rapids, Michigan/Cambridge, U.K., 2006), p.171. Italics original.

answer seems to be that we become glorious when we give glory to another, rather than enjoying the vainglory of self-absorption. Man becomes glorious when he lives for the glory of God, when his life reveals something of the wonderment and delight of the divine. In so far as men and women are created in the image of the God, this must be true of both genders (v.12). But Paul also sees that there is a subsidiary sense in which a woman, in her femininity, uniquely reveals a dimension of human wonderment and delight which the male cannot. Intuitively, we can see this sense of wonder behind the (at first sight) strange wording of the marriage service, in the 1662 Book of Common Prayer, in which the bridegroom vows 'with my body I thee worship'. Moreover, it is expressed in the traditional dress of bride and groom – the bride dressed in the glory of her wedding dress, the groom in sober grey or black.

So there is no contradiction between saying that 'woman is the glory of man' and that 'if a woman has long hair, it is her glory' (v.15, ESV). If this is true, then feminist ideology is a destructive deception, because it understands the 'glory' of a woman as something which needs to be fought for in the assertion of independence and autonomy. The feminist slogan, 'A woman needs a man like a fish needs a bicycle'[2] is a direct contradiction of the multi-layered complementarity and mutuality that Paul sets out in this passage; it actually diverts a woman away from the very possibility of that true glory which comes from the celebration of her femininity, the femininity that is already given by God, and is fulfilled in relationships of godly interdependence and mutuality – in marriage, obviously, but not necessarily limited to marriage. This biblical humanism is inevitably strange to twenty-first century Westerners, steeped in the legacy of Enlightenment rationalism, and perhaps it therefore helps also to state what this sort of godly femininity is not: it is not, on the one hand, the idolatrous and narcissistic glorification of sexuality promoted by the UK's dominant celebrity culture, but neither is it a denial of sexuality in favour of some quasi-androgynous ideal.

Given that cultural expressions of femininity and masculinity will vary, there seems to be no need to insist on head covering as the particular expression of gender difference that was so crucial in Paul's context. But we are not at liberty to ignore the understanding of male

---

[2] First coined by Irina Dunn, Australian writer and politician.

and female which underlies the practice, and which for Paul is clearly universal, being grounded not only in creation but also in marriage, and grounded so profoundly that bridegroom and bride become an eschatological archetype of Christ and the Church. So for a woman to be a bishop is therefore not just to go against the plain teaching of the New Testament, but also to establish a powerful symbolic contradiction of created human identity at the heart of the Church itself. It is in this light that we should look at the specific limits on the ministry of women in public worship which Paul establishes in 1 Corinthians 14:33b-36 and 1 Timothy 2:11-15.

In chapter 11 of 1 Corinthians, women clearly are actively involved in prayer and prophecy so, assuming that Paul is not simply contradicting himself in chapter 14, we should take our cue from the context, which is that of weighing prophecy. That Paul's prohibition is intended to be specifically in this area is also suggested by his reference to the Law in v.34, 'For they are not permitted to speak, but should be in submission, as the Law also says.' (ESV). The natural understanding of 'Law' here is a reference to the Old Testament, given Paul's reference to 'the Law' in his quotation from Isaiah in chapter 14:21. While it is in order for women to prophecy, the weighing of prophecy as a determination of truth and error is an act of governance, and therefore an expression of headship in accordance with the order of creation.

This understanding is reinforced by comparison with 1 Timothy 2:11-15, where the 'silence' of women is directly related to teaching authority. Here, as with Paul's teaching in 1 Corinthians 11, there is a sequence of headship: God – Adam (man) – Eve (woman), in the order of creation. But this time the focus is not the positive one of glory, but a warning that reversing the sequence of headship is symbolic of the great reversal of the fall. Adam had named Eve and should have acted as her protector and guide, but in Genesis 3 Satan addresses Eve rather than Adam, and reverses the sequence of headship, thus: Serpent (Satan) – Eve (woman) – Adam (man). Mike Ovey comments:

> ... having women teach and exercise authority over men symbolically continues the pattern of Genesis 3: it is the pattern of humanity organised in contravention of the original creational order. Conversely, observing Paul's principle whereby men have to assume teaching responsibility symbolically shows men rejecting the sin of Adamic irresponsibility and embracing the original creational order. Paul's principle is, then, that the church manifests the re-

creation of humanity by visibly adopting in symbolic form the creational pattern of Adam's headship over Eve. (Submission to the Rochester Commission 4.3.9).

Reconstructing Jesus

Consecrating a woman as a bishop sets up more than an iconic contradiction of biblical teaching about created human identity. If gender difference is intrinsic to what it means to be male and female in God's image, then this innovation also throws into question the identity of Jesus. If maleness is merely a biological difference and therefore accidental, rather than essential, to the humanity of Jesus, then the consequence seems to be, as John Richardson has cogently argued, that:

> The actual human nature of Jesus of Nazareth as we encounter it in the gospels is, as it were, at one remove from some kind of androgynous and abstract human 'essence'.[3]

That this is indeed the case is suggested by the fact that some feminist theologians feel the need to reinterpret Christ. A recent offering is *Seeking the Risen Christa*, by Nicola Slee who, according to the publishers,

> revisits many of the central narratives of the gospels and key Christological themes, re-imagining them through the eyes and voice of the Christa, offering original and creative perspectives as a resource for theology and spirituality.[4]

If feminists cannot fully relate to Christ without transposing him into the female Christa, where does this plasticity stop? Jesus of Nazareth, as he is presented to us by the gospel writers, cannot be separated from his maleness in his humanity. He is circumcised on the eighth day, he is 'the carpenter, the son of Mary' (Mark 6:3, ESV) whose bloodied and bruised male body is nailed to a cross. Nor can he be separated from his maleness as the second person of the Trinity, the Son whose relates to the Father with that unique intimacy which is a particular characteristic

---

[3] John Richardson, *'Marriage and the Church's ministry – why women bishops don't work for me'*. Unpublished article requested by The Guardian at http://ugleyvicar.blogspot.com/2011/03/marriage-and-churchs-ministry-why-women.html#comments. Accessed 11 April 2011.

[4] Nicola Slee, *Seeking the Risen Christa*, (SPCK, 2011, http://www.spckpublishing.co.uk/shop/seeking-the-risen-christa/). Accessed 11 April 2011.

of John's Gospel. But in the feminist account this Jesus of Nazareth fades from our view. Doesn't what we are seeing and hearing 'through the eyes and voice of the Christa' actually have rather a lot to do with what we are seeing and hearing through the eyes and voice of Nicola Slee? Do we need different Christs for every ethnic group and identity before we can say that 'he died for me'? When we stop receiving Christ in his essential maleness, his humanity becomes obscured and a subject of endless interpretation, as intellectual fashions of human self-understanding come and go. Looked at in the perspective of church history, we are simply seeing a manifestation of an ancient heresy, that of docetism, which emphasised Christ's divinity at the expense of his humanity. Specifically, it saw Christ's manhood as a mere appearance, as a mask behind which the divine essence dwells. The appearance of a man is just that – an appearance. For Bonheoffer, docetism was characteristic of liberal theology because it:

> understands Jesus as the support for or the embodiment of particular ideas, values and doctrines. As a result the manhood of Jesus Christ is in the last resort not taken seriously ... it passes over his manhood and brings Jesus more than ever into the field of speculation and reconstruction.[5]

The *idea* of redemption became much more important than the event, but today, docetism is not confined to liberal theology. It has established again its natural affinity with Gnosticism, in which we might say that a supposed experience of redemption has became much more important than the event itself. In the Early Church, the Gnostic heresy subsumed Jesus into the mystery cults of the ancient world, with their promise of hidden knowledge (*gnosis*) behind and beyond the world of everyday appearance. The parallel, in terms of appearance and substance, with docetic Christology is obvious.

If what we have observed above about Paul's understanding of headship in marriage and the Church is correct, a female episcopate is not only a breach of the direct teaching of Scripture, but also an indirect challenge to orthodox Christology. Without adopting a sacerdotal concept of ordained ministry, we can still say that by entrusting this iconic exercise of 'Christlike' ministerial authority to a woman, the Church invites the assumption that it was indeed cultural accident that

---

[5] Dietrich Bonhoeffer, *Christology*, (Collins, 1966), p.83-4.

the flesh assumed by the Great Shepherd and Bridegroom of the Church was male. Given the rise of new forms of Gnosticism in parts of the Anglican Communion, notably in The Episcopal Church of the United States, but also in England, now is precisely the wrong time to be introducing a model of ministry which opens the door to the docetic Christology of the Gnostics.[6]

Glorifying God

The Anglican commitment to the authority of Scripture, and to interpreting Scripture by Scripture, leads us then to conclude that the limitation of governance roles in the New Testament Church was not simply a reflection of sensitivity to cultural mores of the time. This limitation was intended to be a universally applicable principle, grounded in fundamental creation patterns. Not only is there a complementarity between man and woman – expressed as submission in governance, and patterned on the Trinity itself – but this complementarity is also the key to true femininity, which has the capacity to express in a unique way the glory of humanity as created in the image of God. Given that what primarily distinguishes a bishop from a presbyter is his particular responsibility for exercising governance and his symbolic role, the consecration of women as bishops overturns New Testament order and created order in a uniquely decisive way.

---

[6]   See, for instance, Dave Doveton, *The Way of Balaam; False teachers and the re-appearance of ancient Gnostic beliefs,* (Cadar Press, South Africa, 2010). On 2 May 2011 Manchester Cathedral hosted a 'Spirit of Life' Festival, which imitated New Age practices and included shamanistic healing practices – see Charles Raven, 'Manchester Cathedral: Language, Truth and Magic', in the Church of England Newspaper, 8 April 2011.

4. How does the Church decide? The Trojan horse of Reception

Summary

Evangelical Anglicans, and indeed orthodox Anglicans as a whole, are not defined simply by what they believe, but also by the basis upon which they believe. Unless we take the radically liberal position that religious beliefs are nothing more than human inventions, the content of belief will be, to a greater or lesser extent, something which is received. This chapter considers the following crucial question: how do we recognize what should be received and what should be rejected? Historically, Reception was a process of discerning that which was in accord with what had already been given, supremely through the Scriptures; it is this commitment to historic continuity, governed by the authority of Scripture, which gives historic Anglicanism its character as both Catholic and Reformed.

However, the decision-making process which the Anglican Communion and the Church of England committed themselves to, in discerning the way forward with regard to women's ordination, according to the Grindrod Report for the 1988 Lambeth Conference, amounted to a reversal of the historic pattern. Ten years later the Lambeth Conference commended this process as 'Open Reception', but it may not have been clear that the key value was no longer faithfulness, but 'openness' , much more to do with experimenting with the truth than recognizing the truth. The Oxford Dictionary of the Christian Church which, until the third edition of 1997, had not included an entry for 'Reception', noted tellingly, 'Recently the idea has been used within the Anglican Communion to support experimentation.'

Reception in this guise is neither Catholic nor Reformed. It represents a radical discontinuity with the past and the voice of Scripture is no longer decisive. The Reformers' lively awareness of human fallibility, that even Councils 'may err' (Article XXI), sits uncomfortably with the remarkable confidence that the advocates of 'Open Reception' place in General Synods. The consecration of women as bishops will be not only an outcome of this process, but will also entrench the process itself, leaving the Church of England without any effective defence against further 'Americanisation'. In terms of the principles embedded in 'Open Reception', it is very hard to see what effective barrier there could be to the formal acceptance of clergy and bishops in same-sex unions.

The obvious answer to the question, 'How does the Church of England decide to go ahead with women bishops?', is that it does so through its Synodical structures. But decisions about the nature of ordained ministry and the episcopate are clearly of a different order to much of General Synod's business. These are doctrinal matters which touch on the nature and the unity of the Church itself, to the extent of departing from nearly two millennia of established practice.

There has therefore been a general recognition that something more than voting majorities should be involved, even if that is what it boils down to in the end. That 'something more' is described as the 'process of Reception', which is now the officially sanctioned means by which a decision should be arrived at. So the Lambeth Conference of 1998, in addressing this issue, affirmed in Resolution III.2.b:

> ... for the purpose of maintaining this unity, [this conference] calls upon the provinces of the Communion to uphold the principle of 'Open Reception' as it relates to the ordination of women to the priesthood as indicated by the Eames Commission; noting that "reception is a long and spiritual process". (Grindrod Report)

It is important to ask at the outset what relationship this 'principle of "Open Reception"' bears to the historic practice and understanding of Reception, especially since it is the historic practice and understanding of Holy Orders which are now in question.

The classical practice of Reception

Reception, the act of receiving, is a practice which goes back to the beginning of Christian history, but the ways in which it is exercised make all the difference. In the New Testament we read of gifts being 'received' by those in need, and of people being 'received', that is, welcomed, in circles where previously they were not. Teaching is also 'received', that is, accepted, either as coming from heaven, like the teaching of the Old Testament or the teaching of Jesus, or as being handed on by tradition from reputable authorities in the past. Traditional Jewish teaching is criticized by Jesus as not always being true to the Old Testament, and therefore not suitable to be received, so the apostles substitute a new tradition, derived from Jesus' own teaching (I Corinthians 11:2, 23; 15:1,3; 2 Thessalonians 2:15; 3:6).

In the early Christian centuries, the teaching of Jesus and his spokesmen, the apostles, continued to be transmitted and 'received' in the preaching of the gospel, which was still always open to be checked by Scripture (now including the New Testament as well as the Old). The Scriptures were faithfully expounded by great teachers and misrepresented by lesser ones, and councils of bishops were held to decide controversial questions, if possible, and to condemn dangerous errors. The decisions of councils also needed to be 'received' by the Church at large, or occasionally to be rejected, as with the council of Ariminum in 359 and the so-called Robber Council of 449; the former had endorsed Arianism and the latter Monophysitism. However, four great General Councils in the fourth and fifth centuries upheld orthodoxy and were generally received by Christians. Even after the breach between the Eastern and Western Church in 1054, councils continued to be held on one side or the other of the divide, but were received by that side only. The attempt to hold a council for both sides in Florence in 1438-45 was a failure, its decisions being accepted in the West but rejected in the East. The Church of Rome reckons that Florence was an ecumenical council, despite its rejection in the East, and it takes the same view of other mediaeval Western councils, which were similarly confirmed by the Pope but not received in the East. So it has effectively substituted confirmation by the Pope for general Reception.

The prevailing tendency of councils is conservative, upholding received teaching against modern error. It is not impossible to have a reforming council, when the Church has departed from Scripture, and indeed it is necessary; but the aim of such a council is to bring the Church back to the teaching which it had formerly received. The Church was not born in error, for Jesus is the Truth. On the matter which concerns us at present, the appointment of women as bishops, it cannot be irrelevant that Jesus appointed only men as apostles, since apostles, like bishops, were appointed to be teachers and overseers. He encouraged Mary of Bethany to spend time listening to his teaching, but not to become a teacher (Luke 10:38-42), and he welcomed the women who accompanied him and the apostles on their preaching journeys, but simply as providing material help (Luke 8:1-3). Following Jesus' example, Paul emphasised the headship of men in the congregation (I Corinthians 11:2-16; 14:34-36), and their responsibility for teaching, oversight and leading in prayer (1 Timothy 2:8-15). Thus was established the tradition of having men as bishops and presbyters which later Christian generations almost unanimously received.

Open Reception – open to what?

The modern Anglican concept of 'Reception', whereby the Church is invited to receive unprecedented innovations, which lack convincing support from either Scripture or antiquity, and which have been actually brought into use without general consent, is a revolutionary development. It was thoroughly examined by the late Peter Toon who concluded that:

> No previous effort at reformation or renewal has looked to the future, rather to the settled past. It may even be said that the reformation forward is contrary to every principle of church polity. For the experiment to proceed, it must be permitted by human authority; however, until the experiment succeeds, it cannot be known if the human authorities granting permission have the divinely given authority to allow the experiment.[1]

And we might add that the 'experiment' is hardly a neutral one if it begins with the support of the very body which will eventually have to ratify it, as recent Anglican Synodical practice demonstrates. So the Anglican reinterpretation of Reception amounts to a kind of Trojan horse – the Church risks receiving rather more than meets the eye, because the process implies an acceptance of norms other than Scripture and tradition. It is, for instance, not at all clear that Reception in this form would be any barrier to what has been described as the further 'Americanisation' of the Church – the consecration as bishops of men and women in same-sex relationships, following the pattern now established in The Episcopal Church of the United States.

The first mention of Reception comes in the Grindrod Report produced for the 1988 Lambeth Conference. This Report had been commissioned in response to the announcement by the American Episcopal Church (now The Episcopal Church, TEC), in 1985, that it no longer saw any obstacle to women being consecrated to the episcopate. The Report drew on the experience of the Early Church, the account of the Jerusalem Council (Acts 15) and documents from the patristic

---

[1] Peter Toon, Reforming Forwards: The process of reception and the consecration of women as bishops, Latimer Studies 56/57, 2003.

period, in which the creeds and the canon of Scripture were settled, to argue that the appropriate way to deal with the challenge being thrown down by the American church was a process of Reception, which it described as follows:

> Whenever a matter is tested by the Church there is necessarily an openness about the question. The continuing communion of Christians with one another in faith and worship maintains the underlying unity of the Church while the reception process is at work. The openness needs to be recognized and accepted by those on both sides of the debate. There needs to be openness to the possibility of the new thing being accepted by the Church or rejected by the Church. It also entails a willingness to live with diversity throughout the "reception" process.[2]

The concept was then incorporated into the subsequent Eames Commission Report, before the 1998 Lambeth Conference, and then again into the Lambeth Commission Report, following the crisis which arose with the consecration of Gene Robinson as Bishop of New Hampshire, in November 2003. The 'Windsor Process' was set up as a result, with the purpose of holding the Communion together, despite this radical departure from established norms, but it did not attempt to resolve the specific issue of homosexuality; it was based upon the concept of Reception, which was held to entail mutual restraint and careful listening.

Despite the fact that Reception had now come to occupy such a central place in the official understanding of Anglican ecclesiology, as if it were a principle hallowed by ancient practice, oddly there is no reference to it in the *Oxford Dictionary of the Christian Church* until the third edition of 1997, suggesting that it was the Anglican 'rediscovery' of the concept which prompted its inclusion. Indeed, the entry observes, rather tellingly:

> Recently the idea has been used within the Anglican Communion to support experimentation, e.g. with the ordination of women to the priesthood in some provinces, in the

---

[2] Clause 92, quoted in The Eames Monitoring Group Report, August 1997. http://www.lambethconference.org/1998/documents/report-10.pdf

expectation that such innovations might come to be 'received'. [3]

It would be naïve, therefore, to discount the possibility that Reception in its current Anglican form might owe rather more to institutional convenience than to theological rigour. This is an important question, because if the means by which the decision to go ahead with the consecration of women to the episcopate is flawed, then there must be a strong case for questioning whether that decision itself is right. At the very least, it should not be implemented in such a way as to exile from the Church of England those who disagree.

Open Reception – open to whom?

There are two compelling reasons for thinking that Reception as a process is being abused. The first is that it has become a theological flag of convenience for ideological feminism. The most forceful and superficially appealing argument for the admission of women to the episcopate, without safeguards for those who have conscientious objections – which is exactly where the matter stands at present – is that of simple justice; to limit Holy Orders to males is no better than racism or slavery. Although Galatians 3:28, 'There is neither Jew nor Greek, there is neither slave nor free, there is neither male nor female, for you are all one in Christ Jesus.' (ESV), is pressed into service to support this line of argument, it is not theological but ideological. As has been demonstrated in Chapter 3 above, the theological understanding of equality in the New Testament is much more nuanced, and a process of Reception which maintained the 'openness' urged by Grindrod and affirmed by Eames would surely respect that position. But for ideological feminists, with a feminist reading of Scripture, such 'openness' simply perpetuates injustice.

So it seems that the openness of Reception is also being abused, since it is being deployed in an asymmetrical fashion: the opponents of women's admission to orders must be willing to live with diversity, but proponents are under no such obligation; in fact, their obligation in this case is the reverse, to eliminate diversity. The reason this has not been evident before, of course, is that the admission of women to the

---

[3] *The Oxford Dictionary of the Christian Church*, F. L. Cross, E. A. Livingstone (Editors), 3rd Edition, 1997, p.1371.

presbyterate did not force logic to the surface. It was still possible for the Church of England to muddle along with a mixed economy. It has been possible to work around women priests; it will not be possible to work around women bishops, since all clergy in their dioceses will be under their spiritual authority and there will be no alternative to their ordinations. So, the legislation for women bishops as it currently stands, without provision for dissent, reveals that Reception has been a failed process. It will have enabled the establishment of an irreversible change, under the guise of an experiment, unless current legislation can yet be changed.

Secondly, this abuse of Reception has been possible because the Church of England's ingrained resistance to confessional clarity. This has meant that the concept of Reception has been allowed to overrun doctrinal boundaries, to such an extent that it is no longer clear what things belong to the sphere of 'adiaphora' (things of lesser importance), and so may be changed, and what things are essential for the Church's continued Apostolic and Catholic identity. The actions of TEC and its sympathisers have made this once rather theoretical issue a very practical one.

It is becoming clear, however, that the sexuality issues which have so torn the Anglican Communion are just a manifestation of a deeper conflict about the nature of revelation itself. As the commentator George Conger has recently noted:

> The true issues dividing the church...are becoming clearer. The fight over homosexuality, while still bitterly waged by the combatants, is slowly giving way to a new fight over the nature of truth and divine revelation.[4]

So Gene Robinson and others are advocating the idea that the Holy Spirit can lead us into new truth, which may well depart from established doctrine. This explains TEC's unconquerable confidence that it has a prophetic mission of radical inclusion, which overrides established biblical teaching and morality.

Restoring boundaries

Reception is like a river that has burst its banks and needs to return to its proper channel. As a first step, we should note that the Church of

---

[4] Church of England Newspaper, 24 December 2010.

England is officially committed to the idea that doctrine is something which has already been received. In the *Common Worship* Ordinal, bishops, priests and deacons are all asked a similar question: 'Do you believe the doctrine of the Christian faith as the Church of England has received it ...?' (The Ordination of Deacons). Clearly, if that received deposit is potentially malleable, through the kind of experimentation sanctioned by the Anglican reinvention of Reception, then it is possible to argue that all doctrine is in principle provisional, thereby bolstering the liberal idea that the identity of Anglicanism is much more concerned with the sort of conversation we have than with the doctrines we confess.

The 'in principle' limits of Reception are provided by the Church of England's Canon A5 which states,

> The doctrine of the Church of England is grounded in the Holy Scriptures, and in such teachings of the ancient Fathers and Councils of the Church as are agreeable to the said Scriptures. In particular such doctrine is to be found in the Thirty-nine Articles of Religion, the Book of Common Prayer, and the Ordinal.

The fundamental criterion here is Scripture itself, and the Thirty-nine Articles demonstrate the boundaries within which a process of Reception should work.

Article XX, 'Of the Authority of the Church', states that:

> The Church hath power to decree Rites or Ceremonies, and authority in Controversies of Faith: And yet it is not lawful for the Church to ordain any thing that is contrary to God's Word written ...[5]

So if a substantial body of opinion, as in the present case, argues that a particular experiment is in fact 'contrary to God's Word written' – rather

---

[5] The Church hath power to decree Rites or Ceremonies, and authority in Controversies of Faith: And yet it is not lawful for the Church to ordain any thing that is contrary to God's Word written, neither may it so expound one place of Scripture, that it be repugnant to another. Wherefore, although the Church be a witness and a keeper of holy Writ, yet, as it ought not to decree any thing against the same, so besides the same ought it not to enforce any thing to be believed for necessity of Salvation.

than just being unwise or uncongenial – that should be a very powerful reason for, at the very least, not extending the scope of the experiment.

Furthermore, as was noted in Chapter 2 above, Article XXI, 'Of the Authority of General Councils', recognizes that there is a possibility of error:

> ... (forasmuch as they be an assembly of men, whereof all be not governed with the Spirit and Word of God,) they may err, and sometimes have erred, even in things pertaining unto God.

If even a General Council can be in error, then how much more a Church of England General Synod! If Article XX gives a positive reason for caution, then here we have a negative reason – the humble recognition of our human frailty. Reception can go wrong – indeed the Reformation was in one sense about getting rid of doctrines and practices which had been wrongly received – and this should make us especially cautious about introducing fundamental and irreversible change, especially if there is no general agreement on the biblical warrant for it.

Within the Articles there is, however, a recognition that there is a place for change, and that there can be a legitimate diversity which takes account of different cultural contexts. Article XXXIV, 'Of the Traditions of the Church', affirms that:

> It is not necessary that Traditions and Ceremonies be in all places one, and utterly like; for at all times they have been divers, and may be changed according to the diversities of countries, times, and men's manners, so that nothing be ordained against God's Word.

Again, the criterion of Scripture is central, and this is important in countering an argument that has been put forward by Professor Stephen Sykes,[6] for a more theologically sophisticated form of Reception which does not use Reception merely as a flag of convenience. Building on the Anglican divines' understanding of development, as reflected in Article XXXIV, and Richard Hooker's subsequent defence of the legitimate role of reason against the radical Puritans, according to which the Church is 'both a societie and a

---

[6] Stephen Sykes in *After Eve*, edited by Janet Martin Soskice, (Collins Marshall Pickering, 1990).

societie supernaturall,'[7] Sykes seeks to establish that something which may not be God's will in one era may be so in another. For instance, Hooker is willing to accept that the Reformed Churches of France and Scotland are still valid churches, despite their failure to maintain episcopacy. By extension, Sykes believes that, freed from a culture in which Aristotelian assumptions about women's inferiority held sway, and presented with the evidence of women's full participation in modern society, Hooker would agree that, for a 'societie' existing in a particular culture with its distinct rationality, the ordination of women would be something with which he could concur.

The apparent strength of the argument is that it avoids the implication that, by pressing ahead with women's full admission to Holy Orders, we are somehow exercising a judgment about our forebears in the faith. The subtlety of the argument is that it claims to take a principle from Hooker which arrives, in fact, at a very different conclusion to his sometimes less than flattering estimate of female leadership capacities! But the weakness of the argument is that it ignores the Scriptural principle of Article XXXIV in a way that Hooker's view on episcopacy does not. Whereas there is no direct biblical support for the institution of episcopacy as practised now – or then – there is, at least in its plain sense, clear and direct biblical opposition to the headship of women.

The illusion of optional orthodoxy

In summary, we may say that the recent Anglican practice of Reception is neither Catholic nor Reformed. As a Church which claims to be both Catholic and Reformed, the Church of England is committed to an Apostolic Catholicity, maintaining the historic deposit of the faith in continuity with the Church from earliest times. To act independently of other Churches with a similar claim without very clear Scriptural warrant throws the claim of Catholicity into doubt. As a Reformed Church, the Church of England owes its historic shape and identity to the rolling back of the accretions received by the mediaeval Catholic Church, because they had no warrant from Scripture. So, by the same token, any process of development should have the biblical criteria of the Thirty-nine Articles at its heart. This is manifestly not the case with

---

[7]   Hooker *Lawes* I, xv, 2

the current idea of Reception, which stands church decision-making on its head and becomes a kind of Trojan horse for the values of the ambient culture. If Scripture is determinative of faith and order, the status quo should hold until there is agreement to change. To experiment with fundamental change, before the Church of England has made up its mind, is to concede to the subjective opinions of self-appointed prophets a status which is profoundly corrosive of confessional integrity.

The American theologian, Richard Neuhaus,[8] understood the true nature of such experimentation when he set out his penetrating and brilliant maxim that where orthodoxy is optional, orthodoxy will sooner or later be proscribed – and that is exactly what is now unfolding on both sides of the Atlantic.

---

[8]   Richard John Neuhaus, 'The Unhappy Fate of Optional Orthodoxy' in *The Best of "The Public Square"*, Book Two, (Eerdmans, Grand Rapids, 2001).

5. Seeing things differently - the Biblical pattern for women's ministry in the Church of England

After November 1992, when General Synod had voted for the ordination of women to the presbyterate, an unexpected consequence began to appear. In many Church of England churches, churches in which the authority of the Bible was honoured, and in which there had been deep dismay at General Synod's decision, people began to think afresh about women's ministry. What *should* it be like? What possibilities were there, in Scripture, for women to serve the local church, to use their gifts in God's service? And what should be the *right* relationship between men and women in the Church of Christ?

Re-discovering the Biblical pattern for women's ministry

The starting point had to be the creation story, the setting out of God's design for humanity. Since God has created men and women in His own image – Genesis 1:27 reads, 'So God created man in his own image, in the image of God he created him; male and female he created them.' (ESV) – so, in God's sight, women and men have equal status and dignity.

But since it is *God* who has made men and women different from each other, with different functions and different roles, these distinctions should be respected. The contemporary secular agenda works to abolish such distinctions, and behind the desire to have women bishops there is an emphasis on gender neutrality: 'Whatever a man can do in the church, a woman can do just as well.' But in the debate about women bishops the issue should not be about equal opportunities for women, or about justice towards women. The issue is a *theological* one, and the question should be: 'What is God's will in the matter?'

In the New Testament, when St Paul is giving instructions about how Christians should live together, in the family and in the family of the local church – 'the household of God' (Ephesians 2:19, ESV) – he refers to the creation story, the account of how God has made men and women equal but different. This is the underlying authority for what he writes, and he makes no reference to the culture of his own day.

In recent years, in churches where God's design was respected, and where men were taking the lead according to St Paul's instructions, there was fresh thinking about how to capitalise on this male-female distinction, so that it helped the life of the Church. It was being recognized that some women did have teaching gifts, and that there was a proper context in which these gifts should be exercised.

There was much work for such women to do, pastoring other women through teaching them the Bible, encouraging them and building them up: 'to equip the saints for the work of ministry, for building up the body of Christ,' (Ephesians 4:12, ESV). In particular, they were able to model what it is to live as a Christian woman – in the home, in the workplace, in the local church. No man could do this. The role of older women in this enterprise was also being talked about; it was as though the second chapter of St Paul's letter to Titus (2:3-5) had just been uncovered!

And so various churches began to send women to train for ministry – some for full-time training at theological colleges – and then to employ them full-time. Staff teams were built up, with men and women working together as partners, not competing but collaborating, and playing their different roles effectively.

Partnership among God's people

In order for these teams to work well, a proper understanding of the New Testament teaching on leadership was indispensable. While men needed to recognize that God intended them to lead, women needed to recognize God's intention that they should *let* the men lead, and perhaps encourage them to do so. Though the world was urging women to claim their rights, Christian women needed to see things differently, to see that submitting to their husbands, and submitting to the male leadership of the local church, was a good, dignified and wholesome thing. It was a voluntary action – placing oneself under the leadership of another, an equal – and not at all the same thing as subordination, a word that implies inferiority and also compulsion. As for a model of submission, the highest must be the submission of Jesus to His Father, as He prayed in the Garden of Gethsemane, 'Nevertheless, not my will, but yours, be done.' (Luke 22:42, ESV).

Women who minister in such churches do not feel restricted, but rather, they are fulfilled. One permanent deacon testifies: 'I am most contented when I am allowed to operate within what I understand the biblical foundations to be.' Living and working according to God's design for His Church, within the parameters that He has set, these women are busy and content, glad to be part of a united, harmonious team. And, since 1992, many new jobs have been created for them. (The results of recent research, which bear this out, are given below in *Research findings (1)*.)

The many ways that women can minister to women

In many churches it was a new phenomenon, to have women teaching the Bible to adults. Women teaching children in Sunday School had been normal, but the purposeful teaching of adult women by confident, trained women was new. In Bible study groups of various sizes, in one-to-one conversations and studies, in mother-and-toddler groups, and among students, women were using their teaching gifts to teach the faith, to evangelise, to disciple new Christians, and to support individual women pastorally. In many areas of life, it is more appropriate for a woman to be helped pastorally by a woman, rather than a man: health, marriage, divorce, career path, bringing up children ...

Then, there's the whole area of training: training other women to lead Bible study groups, training them to teach children in Sunday School or to do youth work. In the area of evangelism there were new possibilities: organizing and speaking at events for women, for instance a women's book club, or a women's breakfast. Taking assemblies week by week at the local primary school was another opportunity to serve the kingdom of God.

One woman in ministry, a permanent deacon working in a large church in Cambridge, has written up a week in her life like this:

> In the last week I have met with a group of women and helped them to apply Hebrews 6 to themselves, following a sermon given by a man that they couldn't fully identify with. I met with a young widow grieving the loss of her husband and a student who has an eating disorder. I spoke to a woman who has doubts about the extent of God's love for her, and another who is at a major crossroads in her career and worried about the effect it will have on her children. I prepared two women for baptism and led an enquirers group with a male colleague for men and women investigating the claims of Christ. I also taught Mark 8 to a group of women who are in turn going to teach their student groups what "denying yourself and taking up your

cross" might mean for women living in the 21st century.

No-one can tell me that ministering to these women doesn't constitute a full ministry. I defy you to say that my ministry is inferior to those who minister to men. My male colleagues simply don't have the time, nor is it always appropriate for them to meet with and talk with women in this way.

Training for women in ministry

In recent years a few women have been able to do full-time residential training at a theological college, for three years. In one case, a church sponsored a woman during her training, and gave her a very demanding job when she qualified.

Many women in ministry have benefited from the Cornhill Training Course, started in London in 1991. This pioneering enterprise, which teaches Bible handling skills to women and men, was probably the first training institution in the country to take seriously the differences between men's ministry and women's ministry. The Northern Cornhill (in Sheffield) was set up in 2002, Cornhill Scotland in 2006 and Cornhill Belfast in 2009. The Australian Cornhill has been set up this year (2011).

Working on correspondence courses and attending conferences are other ways of gaining knowledge and training. The Proclamation Trust, which started in the mid-1990s, puts on a conference every January for women in ministry, and between 50 and 70 women attend.

Women's ministry is growing

In Anglican parishes the ministry of women is growing. It is being taken seriously, and churches are getting on with it. In one central London church three women are employed full-time, one of them working with women who work nearby. In Oxford, one church has two full-time women on the pastoral team and one apprentice. And in the City of London, one church has thirteen women in ministry and twelve in training. The value of women's ministry among women is being understood more and more widely, as is the effectiveness of their partnership with male colleagues. (See *Research findings (2)*, below, for recent evidence of this.) In churches where God's design is accepted as being the best, and where the differences between men and women are understood, ministry is vibrant; men are ministering to men, and women to women. There is harmony and completeness, with the diversity that God intended.

Having a woman on the staff of a church is now being seen as essential, not a luxury, and some larger churches are already helping smaller churches to employ women full-time, for pastoral work. Lack of funds, however, prevents more women being employed in this way. The incumbent of a parish in Canterbury diocese wrote:

> In principle, if funds were available, it would be good to have a full-time ladies' worker, who would have plenty of scope in running a monthly club for older people, the weekly Mothers and Toddlers (with a Bible Study group deriving from that – and scope for regular Christianity Explored). That same person would, in principle, have a role in one-to-one work with ladies – and a role with the children's or youth work. As things are, we use a variety of folk in the above roles in a volunteer capacity (most of them ladies). Having a full-time ladies' worker would not make such people redundant – it would give scope for them to be trained better.

A true story

This account appeared in a report by the Revd Carrie Sandom, entitled *Fellow Workers in Christ* and published in 2002, concerning her research into women's ministry:

> One of the ordained women contacted in this research told me of her recent ministerial review. She met with the diocesan adviser for women clergy for over an hour and talked about the work she was involved in, her plans for the future and so forth. At the end of the interview the diocesan adviser said it was the first time she had come across a permanent deacon and was fascinated to hear how contented she seemed to be in that role. She remarked, "I think you are the first ordained woman I have ever met who is not either angry, frustrated or depressed."

> We shouldn't be surprised at this. Those who take God's Word seriously and seek to live it out will prove that what He says in His Word is true and for their good. A growing number of women are committing themselves to the Biblical pattern for women's ministry and are content to live within the parameters God sets them in His Word. Please pray for us as we seek to

live in obedience to Him and point others to the Lord Jesus Christ – in whose service there is perfect freedom.

A better pattern, a better way!

One cannot serve the Church of God unless one first submits to the will of God. If women take hold of the leadership role that God has reserved for *men*, they will be neglecting the role that God has reserved for *them*, which is, ministering to other women and modelling to them the life of a godly Christian woman, things that only women can do.

If a church turns its back on God's design for men and women, in the family and in the Church of Christ, disaster must follow. But when a church orders itself according to the Scriptures, it thrives. There *is* a better way.

Research findings (1): Women's ministry, according to the Biblical pattern, in Church of England parishes - May 2011

Research carried out by email and telephone, in April and May 2011, provides evidence that the ministry of women, according to the Biblical pattern, is flourishing in English parishes.

Thirty-six incumbents, from seventeen dioceses, have described the posts in which women are currently employed in their parishes, in pastoral ministry. The job titles are not standardised, of course, and so the titles given below are only an indication of the work being done. (In a few cases, the number of years a post had been in existence was also supplied.)

Ninety posts are listed below:

Permanent deacon:	3	(one of these is now Associate Minister for Women and Pastoral Care)
Trainer:	1	
Pastoral Worker, or Associate Pastor, or Children's and Family Pastor, or Senior Leader for prayer ministry and pastoral oversight:	18	(in one church, one pastoral assistant works with the elderly, and another with families)
Associate Minister (women's work), or Women's Worker, or Associate for Women's Ministry:	13	(1 post has existed for 10 years, and posts in one church have existed for more than 14 years. From 3 of these churches, in London, a total of 7 women are ministering to women in the workplace)
International Women's Worker:	2	
Women/families and youth and children:	6	
Student Workers:	6	(posts in one church have existed for more than 14 years)
Youth workers, or Chaplain and Youth Minister, or Youth Minister:	8	(1 post has existed for 10 years)
Children's pastors, or children and youth workers:	11	(1 post has been held for 8 years)
Ministry trainees/apprentices:	22	

Research findings (2): Responses from incumbents concerning the pastoral ministry of women on their staff teams

The incumbents who had been invited to provide data, about the numbers of women in pastoral ministry in their parishes, were also invited to comment on the value of employing these women. The responses were invariably positive, and in many cases strongly enthusiastic. They have been grouped under headings; the name of the diocese from which a response has come is given in brackets.

General

'[Her] ministry has made an enormous difference to our work and we wonder how we managed before she started this.' (Chelmsford)

'We're keen to have women working on the paid staff and value their ministry immensely.' (Chichester)

'I need hardly say we value their work enormously.' (Ely)

'... So we value their ministry as highly as male ministry....' (Exeter)

'They both lead services sometimes, so it is seen publicly that the church leadership is not male-dominated.' (Exeter)

'[Having women on the staff] gives recognition to the different gifting of men and women.' (Guildford)

'It would be unthinkable not to have women involved in our ministry team.' (London)

'We are thrilled to have them and they are a vital part of the teams.' (London and Southwark)

'Brilliant!' (Oxford)

'The significance of [her] ministry is indicated by the fact that this has been a long term post; [she] has been on our staff team for over eight years. A well-led children's work has made an important contribution to the steady growth that we have seen over the last 10 years, particularly among families with children. ... I hope too that [her] ministry shows the value that we place on the ministry of women.' (Oxford)

'Excellent! Having women on the staff enriches the ministry. These women are able to reach out to other women and to families more effectively than men.' (Peterborough)

'We currently have 3 ladies on our Ministry Team, fulfilling leadership ministries in various areas of church life – and the leadership team is more complete for their presence.' (Rochester)

'I have worked on three church staff teams which have all included women and have been all the stronger for it. There is so much gospel ministry that is done by them which would not otherwise be done. There are a number of women and children in our church family today who I don't believe would have been reached with the gospel by us were it not for the ministry of the two ... workers who have been on [our] staff.' (Sheffield)

'Both A. and B. are hugely gifted and anointed by God for their ministries. We would be lost without them.' (Southwark)

'We have the best women's worker in the country! She is brilliant with all sorts of people. As Assistant Minister she comes ahead of our two curates in seniority. ... She is busy with pastoral work, teaching and evangelism. ... We are very, very pro-women's ministry.' (Southwark)

The distinctive ministry of women to women

'It's vital that we have women on the ministry team to offer very specific ministry to other women ...' (Bath & Wells)

'Having women on the staff enables us to encourage and train women ...' (Bath & Wells)

'This is the first time we have had a female member of staff - it has been very helpful in showing the women in the church the importance of ministry by women to women, paid or voluntary.' (Chester)

'A female worker is gifted differently and so can do certain things in ministry better than men. [She] can minister to women - when it may not be appropriate for men to do so – [and she] can often relate and minister to women in a more healthy and more effective way than can men.' (Derby)

'At a one-to-one level of discipleship training and instruction, women can read the Bible and pray with women; it would be totally inappropriate for men to read and pray with women. ... In groups, it enables female lay people to be trained to lead. ... It enables discipleship issues specific to women, or, most appropriately handled in single-sex groups, to be addressed more readily.' (London)

'And they [women on the staff] possess sensitivities that men do not have: in particular, they can appreciate the situation of many modern women, who need to juggle the demands of family and work, and who also want to play a part in church life.' (Peterborough)

'[Our women's worker] is in touch with 70-80 women a week. ... Sometimes people come to us in quite a damaged state, and she will nurse them back to spiritual health. ... One valuable aspect of her work has been to train other women, who have gone on to work elsewhere.' (Southwark)

Complementarity

'It's vital that we have women on the ministry team ... [because] they reflect the Biblical complementarity of the sexes within the ministry of the church.' (Bath & Wells)

'Having women on the staff ... also allows us to do this [encouraging and training women] without it seeming to be in opposition to biblical headship: it's complementary.' (Bath & Wells)

'A female worker is a symbolic statement about the equal calling and gifting for ministry of men and women.' (Derby)

Modelling

'Great to have someone to meet up with the teenage girls and be a role model for them. She leads small bible study groups for a number of girls.' (Chester)

'A female worker is able to model ministry by women in a way that encourages and empowers other women in ministry.' (Derby)

'The benefits of having a female member of staff are considerable ... and perhaps more importantly [the benefit] of modelling to the women in the congregation Christ-like living and service.' (Leicester)

'She also helps to encourage women that they can 'do ministry' and gives them a model of how they can do it.' (London)

Adding value to the ministry team

'It's vital that we have women on the ministry team ... because they bring a different dimension to ministry and to our ministry team meetings ...' (Bath & Wells)

'A female worker gives a different perspective on ministry - and life - to men and so including females makes for a more rounded team and fuller perspective.' (Derby)

'Female intuition at staff meetings!' (Exeter)

'At a staff team level, it gives single staff a chance to hear things from a different angle.' (London)

'I immensely value having a woman on the staff team as she brings a different way of thinking and relating to others. She helps to stop us being too competitive and is more sensitive and empathetic than the men tend to be.' (London)

'... I am particularly grateful for her ministry. She has brought a dimension to our Senior Ministry Team which was lacking before. Not only has she been able to develop an effective Bible ministry within the Church, but she has consistently helped us to see things from other angles that otherwise we might have missed.' (Rochester)

Research findings (3): Further testimonies from women in full-time pastoral ministry

'It has been the greatest privilege and joy of my life to teach the Bible and minister to women and children within the biblically ordained role for women   I was ordained as a deacon in the Church of England in 1995 and have served as a permanent deacon in one parish for the last 15 years, having earlier served as a lay member of staff at another church for 5 years. I absolutely love and am completely content in my role of teaching the Bible to women and children; in no way am I unfulfilled. I, and many other women serving in churches in similar roles, have no wish for equality to mean that we have to be in roles identical to men's roles. Rather, we believe we are celebrating the God-given differences between men and women, and serving the Lord as he intended.' (A permanent deacon, Winchester Diocese)

'I am humbled by the way God has used me to serve him in the past. I am in awe of the way God has fashioned my life to bring me to this point of serving him as the Women's Worker in this church. I have never found God and his word wanting to restrict me as a woman.

Rather, his word enables me to be more of the woman he created me to be.

'So I can get on with beavering away, meeting up with women: talking and praying through issues we face as women; opening up the Bible, one-to-one and in our women's groups; learning from those with more experience and wisdom than me, and encouraging older women, as Paul instructed Titus to do, in their invaluable role with younger women. Also, I encourage women to encourage men in their leadership responsibilities! If we want more godly men in our church and families, we need to get on and encourage them! I hope you too recognize the great need for Christian women to be serving God in the church today, and the immense value of what they do.' (A women's worker, Peterborough Diocese)

'I have the great privilege of spending most of my week working alongside male colleagues. Together, we train men and women who hope to be in full-time ministry in the future, and some of the church's small-group leaders. Working under my colleagues' leadership, I help to run extended discussions on bible passages, and on various theological and pastoral topics. It is wonderfully freeing to be able to do this in a way that is distinctively feminine. I also meet up with the women individually, pastoring them more personally. It is one of the highlights of what I do – encouraging them, as women, to engage with God in his word and then seeing them trust him and live out their convictions in the situations where he has placed them, and as they minister to other women. I am thankful daily to the Lord for being able to serve him in this way – I cannot imagine having a role that is more fulfilling.' (A women's worker, with theological training, London Diocese)

Conclusion: The Way Ahead

So where are we now?   After the debates in deaneries and dioceses, the General Synod will debate the Draft Measure in 2012. Two questions remain uppermost in people's minds: is 'provision' needed? If so, what sort of provision is needed?   'Provision' means making arrangements in the legislation for clergy and parishes who have conscientious objections to the principle of consecrating women bishops.   Although some of the leading advocates of the principle of having women bishops believe that any such provision is unacceptable, the Draft Measure does include provision in the form of a Code of Practice.   However, for those who do have conscientious objections to the principle of consecrating women bishops, the proposed Code of Practice route is inadequate:[1] in their view it does not provide them with the security they need. This is the main issue in the debate about the legislation, although many continue to dispute the principle of the acceptability of consecrating women as bishops.   In this concluding chapter, therefore, we will focus on the issue of provision and examine whether there is a better way ahead than the Draft Measure currently being considered.

Why is provision needed at all?

As has been argued in the previous chapters, the first reason is that the principle of consecrating women bishops (and priests) has been, is, and will continue to be a matter of dispute, in the world church, in the Anglican Communion and in the Church of England.   This development has not yet gained the assent of the universal church. Moreover, the grounds on which it is resisted are matters of substance, both theological and ecclesiological, which should not – indeed must not – be lightly set aside.   So, when considering the Draft Measure members of General Synod need to decide whether they accept that the arguments of the opponents to the Measure are substantial matters, matters which should be taken seriously even if one does not actually

---

[1]   A complication here is that, in order to avoid appearing to anticipate Parliament's decision on the Draft Measure itself, the actual Code of Practice is not yet available. An 'illustrative draft' has been presented to the General Synod but it has not been adopted by any authoritative body.

agree with them. It is not inconsistent to be in favour of the principle of consecrating women bishops *and* to believe that the arguments of opponents are substantial enough to be taken into account, when shaping the legislation which will put the principle into effect.

The second reason for believing that adequate provision is required is captured in the expression 'Anglican ethos' – the way in which we characteristically conduct our life as a church. This goes right back to our Reformation origins and the desire to maintain the comprehensiveness of the Church of England, generously understood. As our nonconformist friends (and others) will remind us, we have not always succeeded in achieving that. Nevertheless, Anglicans characteristically aspire to seek to accommodate as many as possible of those who adhere to our confessional position, as set out in the Thirty-nine Articles, while allowing diversity of practice within that framework. We are reluctant to unchurch those with whom we disagree. This necessarily involves debate from time to time about the limits of diversity. But in the present case we are dealing with people whose views on the nature of priesthood and episcopacy were, until twenty years ago, actually *required* of members of the clergy and office-holders of the Church of England. So the argument is that, although the Church of England is changing its position on this aspect of priesthood and episcopacy, our characteristic ethos should lead us to continue to make space among us for those clergy, laity and parishes who cannot go with that change.

The argument for trust

At this point in the discussion, those who are sceptical about the case for provision often argue that the solution lies in trusting our bishops. Bishops can be expected to exercise their ministry with care and sensitivity, particularly with a Code of Practice laying duties and responsibilities upon them. Why is that not sufficient? Four points need to be addressed when considering that question.

First, has the experience of the operation of the Act of Synod and related provisions under the women priests measure – often referred to as 'the two integrities' – been satisfactory? The evidence here is varied, but one fact is very clear: the current Draft Measure explicitly withdraws the provision made under the 1992 Priests (Ordination of Women) Measure, and replaces it with arrangements which most of those who were – and are – opposed to the ordination of women consider less than satisfactory. Although there is dispute about the precise terms of the 'assurances' that were given concerning the binding and continuing nature of the 1992 provisions, the current Draft Measure demonstrates that they can be withdrawn against the will of those for whom they were intended. This simple fact does not engender confidence in the long-term willingness of the church as a whole to accommodate those who cannot in conscience accept the ordination of women priests or the consecration of women bishops. So we need to ask: does the experience of the women priests measure encourage those with conscientious objections to the consecrating of women as bishops to 'trust the bishops'?

Secondly, what has happened in other parts of the Anglican Communion, where women have been admitted to the priesthood and the episcopate? How have those who were opposed to these developments been treated? Sadly, the experience in North America has not been good, with well-substantiated reports of hostile action being taken by bishops and dioceses against clergy and parishes who were opposed, with some cases ending in expensive litigation. The resulting splits among Anglican churches in the United States and in Canada have been extensively reported in the United Kingdom, not least because many parishes and clergy here have strong links with local churches in North America. The issue of women priests and bishops is not, of course, the only cause of these splits; the controversy about sexual ethics has also contributed. But that controversy, too, illustrates how unwilling are many in diocesan leadership in The Episcopal Church of the United States and the Anglican Church of Canada to tolerate dissent. In the Church of England we may not be in the same situation – but it is not surprising that what is going on in another part of the Anglican Communion, with which many have close links, should make the minority in the Church of England even more hesitant to 'trust the bishops' on such questions.

The third point to be considered, when thinking about the adequacy of the Code of Practice route, is people's experience of the operation of other Codes of Practice and similar procedures within the Church of England itself. The two leading examples are the processes under the Pastoral Measure, with regard to the suspension of benefices and the joining together of parishes, and the process under the Patronage Measure, with regard to the appointment of clergy to parishes. A third example would be the operation of clergy discipline. It will be interesting to see whether the new regime, necessitated by widespread lack of confidence in the old processes, will bring significant improvement. The point is simply this: although no-one can be sure how widespread they are, failures by bishops, archdeacons and other diocesan leaders to adhere to the processes are credibly reported, and in sufficient numbers to lead to hesitation about the wisdom of relying upon such procedures, especially in a matter like the consecration of women bishops which is fundamental to the life of the church.

This third point will come as no surprise to many lay people who experience Codes of Practice and similar processes in secular life. While such Codes may work well in cases where there is mutual confidence between the parties, in some areas – such as employment – where that cannot be taken for granted, they are often found to be wanting. Too many cases therefore end up in expensive litigation in the civil courts.

Thus the fourth point to be considered is the application of this form of dispute resolution where matters of conscience and principle are engaged. To work well these Codes of Practice and similar procedures require mutual confidence; they cannot of themselves create such confidence. When things go badly, the way they operate may in fact damage any confidence that did exist. Trust is a powerful dynamic within relationships and organisations, but it needs to be won. And when it has been won, the keeping of it is a continuous task, requiring the engagement of all parties. Has it been won and kept in the matter of women priests and women bishops?

In this book we contend that serious consideration of the above points will lead to the conclusion that the Code of Practice provision in the Draft Measure is an inadequate response to the Church of England's needs when legislating to permit the consecration of women bishops.

What sort of provision is needed?

We must now consider our second question: what sort of provision would be adequate to these needs? In answer to that, two requirements must be acknowledged. The first will have been apparent in the discussion of the case for provision itself: to be adequate and effective, provision must secure the confidence of those for whom it is intended. If part of the objective of making provision is to enable the dissenting minority to remain within the Church of England, then it is vital to establish that the proposals will have that effect.

In practical terms this means acknowledging that the 'dissenting minority' are not a monolithic block (nor, indeed, are the proponents of the legislation). For some, provision is irrelevant: the doctrinal principles involved in the consecration of women bishops are so significant that no form of accommodation of 'dissenters' would satisfy them. On this view the Church of England, when it consecrates women bishops, would be abandoning its claim to be part of the universal one, holy, catholic and apostolic Church. Those who take that view will, sadly, feel forced to move to another church. Thus the Roman Catholic Church has designed the Ordinariate to meet the needs of those of an Anglo-Catholic persuasion. But most 'dissenters' do not take that view and are determined to remain loyal to their Anglican convictions. They are definitely not looking for another church to join: they want to remain members of the Church of England and, given the Church of England's doctrine and ethos, they are expecting that space will be made for them to do so. Understandably, much attention has been paid to the needs of the clergy who hold this view, but it should be noted that very many lay people also share this view.

What, then, do the majority of the 'dissenters' require? As will be evident from the chapters of this book, the heart of the matter is security: the confidence that these 'loyal Anglicans', and their successors, will continue to be accepted as full members of the Church of England, able to hold their views and carry out their ministry in the light of them for the foreseeable future. At heart this has two dimensions: *procedures* – in respect of appointments, vocations, training, teaching and corporate worship; and *permanence* – that the provision should continue, not for a fixed period but until those for whom it is intended consider it is no longer required. A Code of Practice which ultimately depends on the discretion of the diocesan bishop does not meet their needs.

Expressing the situation in this way often provokes the response that what is being asked for is 'a church within a church', and that this would subvert the Anglican understanding of episcopacy, i.e. mono-episcopacy, one bishop for one geographical area, as has been the case since the 1840s. The contributors to this book strongly refute that interpretation. We have shown that authentic episcopal oversight can be, and has been, exercised in a variety of ways, both historically and today. We should not allow ourselves to be trapped in a nineteenth-century, monolithic view of leadership and authority. Two examples conclusively demonstrate the error of that view: historically, monastic and similar orders played a significant role, with their own structures of leadership being separate from but linked to diocesan and provincial structures; and today many dioceses, on account of their size and complexity and notwithstanding the legal theory, require plural leadership by a college of bishops (and others). In short, jurisdiction in practice can be, and is being, shared – for the better government of the church and the proclamation of the gospel.

So we conclude that authentic Anglican ecclesiology *can* accommodate arrangements which would meet the stated needs of those unable, on grounds of conscience, to accept the consecration of women bishops. That understanding led the Archbishops of Canterbury and York to offer their amendment to the Draft Measure in July 2010. Alternatives such as the society model and/or religious orders have also been advocated. No-one pretends that it is easy to find the solution which will meet the needs of the majority who want women bishops and of the minority who find that development unacceptable – and thus enable people of both views to continue to belong to and minister within the Church of England. But it is clear to us that the Draft Measure falls seriously short of what is needed. The health of the Church, and our ability to fulfil our vocation as the Church of England, requires further work to craft a more acceptable way forward, one based not on mere pragmatism but on sound theological and ecclesiological foundations.

We therefore ask the readers of this book to pause and reflect before endorsing the current Draft Measure to allow the consecration of women bishops. As the following motions[2] which have been passed in a number of dioceses illustrate, approving this legislation is not the only way ahead. There is a better way; let us give the Holy Spirit the opportunity to enable us to find it.

PHILIP GIDDINGS

READING, OCTOBER 2011

---

[2] The text of the Following Motion proposed by the Church of England Evangelical Council, and the text of the Archbishops' Amendment Motion, follow this page.

I. Following Motion from the Church of England Evangelical Council

This synod

1. desires that all faithful Anglicans remain and thrive together in the Church of England; and therefore

2. calls upon the House of Bishops to bring forward amendments to the draft Bishops and Priests (Consecration and Ordination of Women) Measure to ensure that those unable on theological grounds to accept the ministry of women bishops are able to receive episcopal oversight from a bishop with authority (i.e. ordinary jurisdiction) conferred under the Measure rather than by delegation from a Diocesan Bishop.

Autumn 2010

2. Archbishops' Amendment Motion

'That this Synod [i.e. the Diocesan Synod] request the General Synod to debate a motion in the following form:

"That this Synod [i.e. the General Synod] call upon the House of Bishops, in exercise of its powers under Standing Order 60(b), to amend the draft Bishops and Priests (Consecration and Ordination of Women) Measure in the manner proposed by the Archbishops of Canterbury and York at the Revision Stage for the draft Measure."'

Appendix 1: Submission to the Commission on Women in the Episcopate

The Economy of Salvation and Ecclesiastical Tyranny: Issues Relating to Female Episcopacy – Dr Michael J. Ovey

What follows is, with minor corrections, a copy of a submission to the Commission which looked at the possibility of female bishops. The original format has been retained so that readers know precisely what arguments were before the Commission and can therefore evaluate the extent to which these are addressed or answered.

The argument falls broadly into two parts, first, an examination of the economy of salvation, so often urged as a way of de-privileging the texts of 1 Timothy 2:11-15 and 1 Corinthians 14:33b-36. The conclusion here is that it is exactly the economy of salvation that shows the traditionalist case is right. The second broad area of discussion deals with what lies behind the particular question of female bishops, namely the more general issue of how a denomination copes with a question of this kind. The analysis pursued here explains our denomination's actions using a venerable and powerful, if controversial, analytical tool, that of 'ecclesiastical tyranny' (see 6.2.13-15, 7.2 and 7.3), albeit exercised in our context with a certain genteel finesse. It is not easy to feel optimistic that this analysis will be squarely faced. To accept the possibility that one may be behaving tyrannically (see the definition in 6.2.15) is demanding not merely intellectually but even more so emotionally, especially for an institution which so strongly mirrors English social attitudes towards the suave exercise of power.

Nor is it easy to feel optimistic that these arguments will commend themselves to some evangelicals. It is tempting to feel that all is safe in one's own parish, for one's own time, perhaps comforted by the notion that 'A bishop is an estate agent'. Quite apart from undervaluing the biblical material and its concern about preventing false teaching in the church (see 2.2 and 2.3), this overlooks several facts: the 'estate agents' will have an influence in who is appointed to which parish, and in the organisation and grouping of parishes, as well as, of course, in the selection of future ordinands and their training. Further, the ecclesiastical tyranny displayed on this issue will be available for use on others. When a denomination adopts the tools of ecclesiastical tyranny, there are no 'safe' parishes – not in the long run. The recent treatment of Charles Raven and his congregation in Kidderminster has made examination of this area even more pressing.

Submission to the Commission on Women in the Episcopate – Dr Michael J. Ovey.[1]

I. Introduction

1.1 *The object of this paper is to provide a submission exploring:*

- the theological context of the consecration of women to the episcopate;

- the exegesis of relevant texts within that context; and

- some of the arguments pertaining to justice and Reception.

2. Episcopacy in the context of the church

2.1 *The nature of the church as the recreated humanity*

2.1.1. Irenaeus of Lyons remarks '... the whole economy of salvation regarding man came to pass..., in order that God might not be conquered, nor His wisdom lessened...'.[2] Here Irenaeus paraphrases and extends the thought of Ephesians 3:10 ('...through the church the manifold wisdom of God might now be made known to the principalities and powers in the heavenly places.') and also sets a theocentric context within which Christian theological reflection, including that on the episcopate, must be set.

2.1.2. The context of Ephesians 3:10 shows how the church, the fruit of the economy of salvation, makes God's manifold wisdom known. In chapter 2 Paul has dwelt on the human predicament both in terms of rebellious estrangement from God (Ephesians

---

[1] This paper was submitted to the Bishop of Rochester's commission exploring the theology and practical implications of allowing women to be bishops in the Church of England.

[2] Irenaeus, *Against Heresies* III.23.1.

2:3, 12) and from one another (Ephesians 2:14, where reciprocal human estrangement is emblematised by the hostility between Jew and Gentile). Such a predicament is a disastrous perversion of the original ordered cosmos of Genesis 1 and 2, in which there was a single human race under the sovereignty of God. The events of Genesis speak of a humanity that rejects the benevolent sovereignty of God as it takes the fruit of the tree of knowledge and whose mutual relations also experience dysfunction, most notably of course in the events of Genesis 4.

2.1.3.   This now disordered cosmos casts doubt on the wisdom of the Creator. For the Creator has called into being a cosmos that does not, it seems, reflect His order. He has spoken, and it is, apparently, not so. The church, however, vindicates God for it is one humanity (Ephesians 2:15), restored to God (Ephesians 2:16) and at peace with itself (Ephesians 3:6).[3] The church, then, vindicates God's creative work in two respects:

(a)   She is humanity once more under the headship of the creative Word, the Son of God. She therefore manifests this in her obedience to the commands and laws God has revealed, for here she does what Adam and Eve did not.

(b)   She is a single humanity, whose members are related to each other within the framework of their own relationships with the triune God. She manifests this by her rejection of the barriers between humans that sin has brought – racism, classism, nationalism and sexism.

2.1.4.   In this way, then, we rightly speak of redemption as re-creation,[4] as Athanasius observes,[5] for God's original work in creation has been successfully recapitulated, to use the terms of Irenaeus. We are also left with underlying principles which go beyond the difficulties often observed in drawing out a normative form of church government from the New Testament material. A form of church government clearly cannot contradict explicitly, or even implicitly, the theocentric and eschatological nature of the church as the community of redeemed and re-created humanity.

---

[3]   On this see O'Brien *The Letter to the Ephesians* (Grand Rapids: Eerdmans) 1999:246.
[4]   Note 2 Corinthians 4:1ff; 5:17ff. See too Romans 8:19-23.
[5]   De Incarnatione 6 & 7.

Thus a form of church government must manifest the re-createdness of God's people:

(a)   in its obedience to Christ as Lord and head; and

(b)   in its unitedness as a single humanity under Him.

These are two fundamental parameters within which the question of women of episcopacy must be discussed.

2.2 *The Church in her eschatological setting: the Scriptures and false teaching*

2.2.1. However, while the church indeed now vindicates God's manifold wisdom, she does not yet do so perfectly. She is, of course, eschatologically conditioned in that God's work in her has been started but not yet completed. God's work in his people has indeed been sealed with the Holy Spirit (Ephesians 1:13), but full possession lies in the future. This particular eschatological condition raises two issues amongst others.

2.2.2. *First,* sin and error will persist in the as yet unperfected church. Paul adverts to this in Acts 20:29f and John envisages it in 1 John 1:8. Luther famously observed that a believer was *simul justus et peccator* (at the same time justified yet a sinner) and the church as a body of believers may thus fairly be said to be *simul justa et peccatrix.* This reality is recognized in Article XIX of the XXXIX Articles and underlies the limits on the authority of the church set out in Article XX.

2.2.3. *Secondly,* the rule of Christ must be realised in this as yet unperfected church. Paul points out in Ephesians 4:7-16 that Christ has indeed made provision for this. He has provided apostles, prophets, evangelists and pastors and teachers to equip His people. O'Brien aptly comments 'Those listed are ministers of the Word through whom the Gospel is revealed, declared and taught.'[6] Christ rules His people through His Word, and it is this Word which builds them into maturity under Him and which protects them from 'every wind of doctrine' (Ephesians4:14). Hence again the position of the XXXIX Articles in their stress on the supremacy of Scripture (Article VI) and the

---

[6]   O'Brien 1999:298.

necessity of instruction from 'the pure Word of God' in the visible Church (Article XIX). Nor is this an antiquarian position: it was, of course, re-affirmed in the Lambeth Quadrilateral of 1888 (The Scriptures are 'the rule and ultimate standard of faith'). In terms of the current debate the 1990 Report *Episcopal Ministry* speaks of Scripture as 'the normative and primary witness' (paragraph 26), while the 1998 Lambeth Conference '...reaffirms the primary authority of the Scriptures...' (Resolution III.1.a).

2.2.4. This concern with true instruction by a ministry of the Word is a recurrent theme in the New Testament. It is especially noticeable in the Pastoral Epistles and the Johannine correspondence as well as 2 Peter and Jude. Timothy and Titus are to prevent false teaching (e.g. 1 Timothy 1:3) and install those who will give healthy instruction (Titus 1:5-9). Christians are enjoined not to support false teaching (2 John 10-11).

2.2.5. Indeed, the New Testament contains some sobering reflections on false teaching:

(a) Paul foresees that it will emerge from **within** the body of teaching elders (Acts 20:30). As such institutional succession, even where one has been appointed by an apostle, is no final guarantee of spiritual health.

(b) Paul sees clear limits on what even an Apostle may preach and do (Galatians 1:8f; 2:11ff). The most exalted office does not entitle one to alter the tradition.

(c) Paul envisages the **success** of false teaching (Acts 20:30, in which false teachers acquire disciples and 2 Timothy 4:3ff where people choose false teachers to 'suit their own likings'). On this basis, acceptance of a particular strand of thought is not a reliable indicator of its Christian faithfulness.

2.2.6 Moreover, the early church reproduced exactly this priority. Thus Ignatius of Antioch,[7] so strongly associated with an elevated view of the episcopate, stands equally emphatically against false teaching (e.g. *To the Trallians* 6). In fact Ignatius is

---

[7] Traditionally held to have been martyred in 107 A.D. His letters seem largely to have been written *en route.*

so insistent on the role of the bishop precisely because that safeguards the people against false teaching (e.g. *To the Trallians* 7, *to the Philadelphians* 2). The bishop's place is no mere hierarchical supremacy but genuinely a servant role in his protection of the people of God. There again *Didache* 11-13 (probably brought into its final form before 150 A.D.) lays out the necessity of discretion and testing when it comes to itinerant preachers. Their apparent provenance or reputation is not the issue. Athanasius, of course, insisted that arianising bishops were no true successors to the Apostles, no matter how unimpeachable the institutional transmission might be.

2.2.7 It is against this context of the need to avoid false teaching and the difficulties of doing so that emerging Episcopal responsibilities must be considered.

2.3 The emerging place for episcopal responsibility in New Testament churches

2.3.1. As stated above, there are difficulties in setting out a normative form of church government from the New Testament. A primary difficulty has been in discerning a position of bishop (*episkopos*) which is clearly differentiated from that of priest/presbyter (*presbuteros*). Titus 1 with its arguably interchangeable terminology in 1:5 and 7 is the *locus classicus*. It would, however, be simplistic to infer from this that the New Testament knows only the orders of presbyter/bishop and apostle. The reason for this is precisely the role played by Timothy and Titus within Paul's apostolic care for churches.

2.3.2. Titus is left (Titus 1:5) to complete what is undone, which is closely linked to the appointment or ordination of presbyters in every town. Responsibility for the appointments is left with Titus himself, but it must be noted that Titus does not have *carte blanche*. His discretion is fettered by the need to choose men of good conduct and who are personally committed to what they have been taught. These men must be able to refute false teaching and uphold the truth – the characteristic emphasis on the importance of avoiding false teaching that was noted above.

2.3.3. Titus himself is not immune to the charge to give sound teaching (Titus 2:1, 7b) as well as to provide an example of godliness of life (2:7a). His character is to be that of a presbyter, but he appears to have a jurisdiction going beyond that of a local congregation of believers (note the 'every town' of 1:5). Paul certainly envisages him as having a real authority (2:15), but this must rest on his providing faithful teaching, since Paul does not accept heterodoxy amongst presbyters. How much less in one who appoints them.

2.3.4. To this extent several features require note:

(a) the existence of a jurisdiction of appointment going beyond the local congregation;

(b) the genuine authority adhering to that jurisdiction;

(c) the necessity of ruling on the orthodoxy or otherwise of someone's belief and teaching for the sake of ruling on their fitness as a presbyter;

(d) the overall framework of the necessity of orthodox rather than heterodox instruction; and

(e) the lack of any statement that Titus by virtue of his appointing function is the focus of unity for the churches on Crete – rather, unity between the churches is implicitly provided by their faithful holding to a common faith.

2.3.5. In the case of Timothy at Ephesus, there are indications that a presbyterate is already in place (1 Timothy 5:17). However, this can scarcely be called a particularly effective presbyterate since Ephesus presents problems of false teaching (1Timothy 1:3, 7 and 6:3ff). Indeed, conceivably members of the local presbyterate were themselves the problem (possibly referred to in 6:5, and as Paul had foreseen in Acts 20:30). Since the local presbyterate has failed in just the kinds of presbyteral tasks Paul outlines in Titus of preserving the people of God from false teaching, it is no surprise to find that Timothy's charge is to supplement the local shortcomings and prevent false teaching (1 Timothy 1:3). This naturally suggests a real authority.

2.3.6. It is perhaps easy to overlook the implications of 1 Timothy 1:3. The Ephesian church and its presbyterate obviously had an excellent institutional heritage (from Paul himself), and in fact have the same institutional pedigree as Timothy himself. To that extent there is no question of its institutional legitimacy. The fact of common institutional bond, though, does not provide a satisfactory basis for unity, in Paul's view. If it did, the final warning of 1 Timothy 6:20f would not be warranted. Yet for Paul that institutional provenance is not enough. He considers that the existence of false teaching not merely excuses but requires intervention.

2.3.7. Similar personal demands are made of Timothy as were of Titus. He is to be of godly teaching and personal life (1 Timothy 4:12 and 16). He stands apart to some extent from local presbyters because he has been sent in with a particular task. In that sense his role carries within it the seeds of a supra-local jurisdiction, and this is especially so if Ephesus contained, as some have argued, a number of local congregations by this time.

2.3.8. This tends to present a similar task profile to that of Titus':

(a)   a jurisdiction which is not purely local, this time of regulation of an existing teaching situation and presbyterate;

(b)   genuine authority;

(c)   the necessity of ruling on someone's orthodoxy for the sake of regulating what is taught in Ephesus;

(d)   the overall framework of the necessity of orthodox rather than heterodox instruction; and

(e)   the lack of any statement that Timothy provides the focus of unity for the Ephesian Christians – rather, common knowledge of the one truth provides that.

2.3.9. In this way, the New Testament provides evidence of an embryonic supra-local jurisdiction, relating to the appointment and regulation of teaching in the local churches. The rationale for this is clear: the need to preserve the people of God from false teaching, at times possibly even from its own presbyterate. In this way, Titus and Timothy minister to local churches without being simply further presbyters of those churches. Our own recent experience of the 'Nine O'Clock Service' in Sheffield illustrates the wisdom of this. For there a local congregation did not find internal regulation possible because of the psychological ascendancy of the leading priest over the congregation. What this requires of the Timothy/Titus figure is a clear and faithful grasp of the message once for all transmitted from the Apostles and the ability to rule on whether or not a particular teacher is orthodox or not.

2.3.10. This is the kind of understanding of the bishop's task that is to be found in the Book of Common Prayer. In the course of the Consecration service the bishop-elect or archbishop-elect avers that Scripture contains 'sufficiently all doctrine required of necessity for eternal salvation through faith in Jesus Christ', and that he is 'ready, with all faithful diligence, to banish and drive away all erroneous and strange doctrine contrary to God's Word; and both privately and openly to call upon and encourage others to the same'. In terms of personal life, one of the closing prayers for the consecrated bishop or archbishop is that he 'may be to such as believe a wholesome example, in word, in conversation, in love, in faith, in chastity, and in purity...'. This reproduces, of course, the Pauline thought that Timothy and Titus must watch their lives and doctrine. There may no doubt be more that a bishop may properly do within an Anglican social and cultural context, but there can hardly be less, if New Testament priorities are to be observed.

2.3.11. This kind of understanding continues in the present. Thus the 1990 *Episcopal Ministry* Report is happy to head paragraphs 369-380 with the heading 'The bishop as guardian of faith and order'. The Virginia Report comments in similar vein in paragraph 3.17.

2.3.12. This kind of understanding of episcopal responsibility must now be considered in the light of the re-created united humanity and against the texts bearing on the role of women. To this we now turn.

3. *Galatians 3:28 and the re-created united humanity*

3.1 *Galatians 3:28 and the abolition of distinctives*

3.1.1. It has been suggested that Galatians 3:28 contains a dominant theme for Christian theology, a seminal insight into the new humanity, and one quite in keeping with the considerations of 2.1.4. above. The racial and social distinctives that separate humans from one another and fracture the original created unity of humanity are overcome in Christ. To insist on continuing distinctives of this type is to deny what Christ has done in renewing humanity. One such distinctive that Galatians 3:28 sets out is that of male and female.

3.1.2. On this basis, to deny women ordination to the presbyterate or consecration to the episcopate is obnoxious in the extreme, for it stands on the same theological level as ethnocentrism or classism. It is a denial of the effects of the Gospel.

3.1.3. This formidable argument needs careful analysis. First, naturally, it must be examined contextually. Some controversy exists over the precise nature of the Galatian problem.[8] The issue is certainly one of seriousness, for Paul charges the Galatians with turning to a different Gospel (Galatians 1:6) and the critical issue relates to the keeping of the Jewish Law (Galatians 3:2 and 5:2), apparently as a condition for being heirs to the Abrahamic promise (Galatians 3:7). Paul has, though, encountered similar issues elsewhere, and here the incident at Antioch recounted at Galatians 2:11-21 proves illuminating.

3.1.4. At Antioch, Peter and Barnabas had withdrawn from table fellowship with the Gentiles (Galatians 2:12). Paul analyses this as failing to act in conformity with the Gospel, because it forces the Gentiles to judaise. The implicit message of Peter's actions is that the Gentiles are not truly of the people of God without judaising. Such enforced judaising, Paul reasons, undercuts the sufficiency and necessity of Christ's work (Galatians 2: 21). In this sense Paul's concern is not just over how someone must be saved but also over the place and adequacy of Christ as a saviour.

3.1.5. Similar considerations apply to the Galatian problem. In chapter 3 the presenting question is, Who are the children of Abraham (3:7)? That is, Who inherits the Abrahamic promises? Paul's argument is that men and women are made righteous by faith in Christ, not legal observance (3:11ff), since Christ becomes cursed for our sakes (3:13). On this basis the blessing given to Abraham falls on Gentile believers too. The consistent stress is on Christ and the sufficiency of his work. Paul goes on to say that this marks no change of plan on the part of God. The Abrahamic promise, which he has set out as a covenant of grace not law (3:6), is God's first and constant plan for human salvation (3:15-19), and the Law was added as a measure for sin's

---

[8] Notably over the validity of the so-called New Perspective on Pauline studies associated with E.P. Sanders.

sake until the coming of Christ (3:19ff). Thus Paul asserts there is neither Jew nor Greek, bond nor free, male nor female in the context of who inherits the blessing of Abraham, and on what grounds.

3.1.6. This means that to violate the principle of Galatians 3:28, one must be asserting a difference between human groups which impliedly undercuts the adequacy and necessity of Christ's work in making us heirs of Abraham. It is very far from obvious that this is the case in the question of consecrating women to the episcopate. To ascertain whether this is in fact so it is necessary to look at other considerations relating to the unity of the new humanity.

3.2 The new humanity: unity and uniformity

3.2.1. The unity of the new humanity is not to be confused with uniformity. Paul's use of the body metaphor for the church in, inter alia, 1 Corinthians 12:12-30 shows a body which is united but diverse. In fact Paul seems to speak against uniformity of ministry (vv. 29-30). To that extent, diversity of ministry amongst believers is compatible for Paul with the principles of Galatians 3:28.

3.2.2. Furthermore, the diversity of function does not mask a difference of value, for vv 21-26 speak of the due place of each member of the body and in particular verse 25 calls for an equal concern for each part. In this sense Paul endorses diversity of function but demands equality of value. This consideration is reinforced by the idea that our value or worth is conferred by the price Christ paid for our redemption (1 Corinthians 6:19, 20. Compare 1 Peter 1:18, 19). For these reasons it is simplistic to conclude that the allocation of functions to a particular group necessarily speaks of inequality of value.

3.2.3. In fact, the Pauline corpus contains material that does speak of gender differences amongst believers. One obvious example is the continued depiction of practising homosexuality as sinful (Romans 1:26-27, 1 Corinthians 6:9), which is only intelligible if gender is retained. A further example is the different roles of husband and wife in marriage, in which a husband is commanded to love his wife with a love modelled on the sacrificial love Christ shows the church (Ephesians 5:25), while the wife is to obey her husband (Ephesians 5:22).

3.2.4. This latter example requires development, both because it is dealing specifically with the question of ordered relationships between the sexes, and because such strenuous efforts have been made to deny a relationship of authority and submission between husband and wife.

3.2.5. Thus, in the case of the Ephesians 5:21-33 passage, it has been suggested that the key verse is verse 21 which introduces the entire section on household relationships (5:21-6:9). This speaks of submission to one another, and accordingly the case is made that Paul has mutual submission in view here, that is to say each submits to the other, each preferring the other's good. This argument receives further support from an appeal to the Trinitarian nature of God, in which each divine Person looks to the others – for the Trinity is a community of other-person centred Beings.

3.2.6. However, the argument for mutual submission suffers from a number of defects. First, it arbitrarily limits the semantic range of the word normally translated 'each other'/ 'one another' in verse 21 (*allelois*). The mutual submission argument takes this word as meaning strictly reciprocal submission. In fact, the range of meaning for *allelois* is wider and does not always entail strict each-to-each reciprocity, although it may. It covers cases where people are being designated within a group and within that group there are mutual relations. It is thus used (Revelation 6:4) to talk of men killing one another, but it is hardly to be thought that there is perfect symmetry in that each kills the one who kills him. English captures this nuance by the phrase 'one another' (in fact the NIV's translation of Ephesians 5:21) rather than 'each other'. On this basis, it must be tested whether 'each other' (strict reciprocity) or 'one another' is the correct translation for *allelois* in verse 21.

3.2.7. Secondly, the argument for mutual submission produces eccentric ecclesiological results. For Paul goes on to compare (5:23) the marital relationship with that of Christ and the Church. If there is mutual submission between husband and wife and Christ is a husband, then it follows that he is in a relationship of mutual submission with the Church. This is, to put it mildly, at odds with the description of Christ in Ephesians 1:10 and 20-23 which envisages Christ as cosmic king under the appointment of the Father. This, then, suggests that 'each other' (strict reciprocity) is not the correct translation for verse 21, but 'one another' is.

3.2.8. This consideration is strengthened by other factors. Consistent application of the strict mutual submission interpretation would apply to other material in Paul's table of 'house rules' in 5:21-6:9, notably the parent-child relationship. This stands significantly at odds with the biblical understanding elsewhere, which envisages children obeying their parents and being blessed for doing so. To say the least, there are circumstances where it is positively dangerous for a child to have his or her parent submit to him or her. A further point that is often made here is that the idea of strictly reciprocal submission is a logical nonsense. It is different from, say, bearing one another's burdens where reciprocity is possible, for submission involves obeying another person and one does not obey another where that other obeys oneself. The riposte could be made that this is more a paradox than a nonsense. Yet this is open to the further objection that this is merely a rhetorical device to evade the gravity of the objection. Granted that paradox may exist, it does not follow that it should be lightly invoked to justify an interpretation which is, on other grounds, unattractive.

3.2.9. The overall New Testament context renders the strict reciprocity construction of Ephesians 5:21ff still less viable. Paul has further 'house rules' material in Colossians 3:18-4:1 and Titus 2:3-10. In both cases, the commands to husbands and wives are asymmetrical, with wives being commanded to obey their husbands, but not vice versa, although husbands are commanded to love their wives. A similar pattern is found with 1 Peter 3:1-7 – the perspective is not simply Pauline. At this point one realises that the strict reciprocity construction starts to read different parts of the New Testament in opposition. This is, of course, forbidden by Article XX which enjoins Anglicans not to construe different parts of Scripture repugnant to one another. On this basis, the strict reciprocity construction adopts an un-Anglican interpretative strategy.

3.2.10. For all these reasons, then, the strict reciprocity construction of Ephesians 5:21 ('each other') must be adjudged a clear failure and the appropriate translation of 'one another' adopted, in which Paul sets out in 5:21 the general idea of submission in various relationships which he then develops in specific detail in the following verses.

3.2.11. It has also been suggested that Paul does not in fact intend obedience in Ephesians 5:22 or Colossians 3:18. This rests on the use of the word *hypotasso* in these verses rather than *hypakouo* as in Ephesians 6:1 (children) or 6:5 (slaves). Accordingly, the apt translation is not 'obey' but rather 'respect'. Here the idea is that there is clear blue water, semantically speaking, between *hypotasso* and *hypakouo*. In fact, such a distinction seems untenable. Thus in Titus 2:5 and 9 *hypotasso* is used in both instances, the former dealing with wives, the latter with slaves, while elsewhere Paul uses *hypotasso* in a sense requiring obedience (e.g. Romans 8:7 and 10:3). Outside the Pauline corpus, Peter initially uses *hypotasso* of a wife's attitude to her husband (1 Peter 3:1, 5) but develops this with the example of Sarah who relates to her husband in terms of *hypakouo*. There is, then, clear semantic overlap between the terms, and within the range that these verbs bear, the notion of obedience is to be included because of the comparison drawn in Ephesians 5:22ff between marriage and the relationship of Christ with his Church. Obedience is appropriate in that context.

3.2.12. In terms of the Trinitarian appeal of 3.2.5 above, some care must be exercised here. It is relatively uncontentious that the Persons of the Trinity relate to each other in an 'other-person centred' way. It is far more contentious that this implies an egalitarian Trinity. A fundamental of Trinitarian theology has been that the economic Trinity (the Trinity as it acts in the economy of creation and redemption) reveals the immanent Trinity (the Trinity as it is in eternity). This has been the historic view of the church, forcefully formulated by Tertullian (*Against Praxeas*), adopted by Athanasius on the basis of John 14:6-11 (*Against the Arians*) and recently re-articulated by K. Rahner.

3.2.13. Yet, as has often been observed, the economy of salvation and creation shows us a Son and Spirit who do the Father's will. Accordingly, applying the principle that the economic Trinity reveals the immanent, the economy shows us a three-personed godhead where the eternally begotten Son and breathed Spirit are in a relationship of order. They are not inferior at the level of being – the explanatory words at the end of the original Nicene Creed[9] make that clear, for they are of one being with the Father. This is confirmed by the way 1 Corinthians 15:28 sees the Son ultimately referring all authority back to the Father, and, indeed, in the view of many, by 1 Corinthians 11:3.[10]

3.2.14. On this basis the Trinitarian appeal of 3.2.5 seems to rest on what remains, to put it no higher, a controversial version of Trinitarian theology. It is therefore a dubious step simply in terms of method to use this somewhat controversial version of Trinitarian theology to provide leverage to displace the traditional analysis of marriage as an asymmetrical relationship in which there is not only love but also obedience.

3.3   Is headship in marriage purely a result of the Fall?

3.3.1. It is, though, sometimes suggested that this analysis of marriage is one which is purely a result of the Fall, and that it is therefore mistaken to have provisions made because of the Fall perpetuated within the redeemed community. Appeal is sometimes made to Genesis 3:16, with the argument that it is only here that a husband's headship is introduced. This, then, is the question, whether a husband's headship pre-dates the Fall.

3.3.2. This takes us to an examination of Genesis 2 and the creation of woman. It is worth observing that Genesis 2:18 does not necessarily speak of ordered relationship between husband and wife in its use of the term 'helper', for a helper may be a superior (God is the helper of Israel). The term translated 'fit for

---

9   The relevant words which explain 'of one being' (*homoousios*) read: 'And whosoever shall say that there was a time when the Son of God was not or that before he was begotten he was not, or that he was made of things that were not, or that he is of a different substance or essence [from the Father] or that he is a creature, or subject to change or conversion – all that so say, the Catholic and Apostolic Church anathematizes them.'

10   The controversy over 1 Corinthians 11:3 is whether the headship language applies to the immanent relation. It is difficult to see why it does not, without either severing the economic-immanent link, or adopting a kenotic or nestorianising christology. The latter Athanasius sees as ruled out by John 14:6-11, the former has been prohibited by the Chalcedonian Formula of 451. G. Fee takes a different view – *The First Epistle to the Corinthians* (Grand Rapids: Eerdmans) 1987:505 – but without adverting to the christological difficulties his view creates.

him' does not necessarily betoken ordered relationship either, although it may well denote both similarity but difference – complementarity, so to speak, but not woman as an exact doublet of man.

3.3.3. Genesis 2:23 does though recount the man (*ish*) determining that the female be called woman (*isshah*). Now there are reasons for thinking this does involve a relationship of authority or responsibility. Man has earlier named the creatures (Genesis 2:19) and this is apparently linked to the notion of dominion the man has been given. Further, later in the Scriptures, naming is seen to be a significant activity, associated obviously with identity and also lordship – God *names* Abram as Abraham, and Jacob as Israel, both within the context of his relationship with them as their God. Wenham sums it up thus: 'Though they are equal in nature, that man names woman (cf. 3:20) indicates that she is expected to be subordinate to him, an important presupposition of the ensuing narrative (3:17).'[11]

3.3.4. This interpretation has not been without criticism. Thus Atkinson argues that 2:23 does not involve order, because the 'standard naming formula' is not used.[12] However, the putative naming formula to which he appeals occurs only three times, and with some variety. This is a slender basis on which to build a 'standard naming formula'. Moreover, the Greek Old Testament gives little or no indication of difference between the namings of 2:19 and 23, both of which employ simply the verb 'I call' (*kaleo*). There is, further, no marked difference between the terms of Genesis 2:23 and 3:20, where the woman (*isshah*) is named Eve after the Fall, a situation where, on the view under discussion, there is headship between husband and wife. Rather, Atkinson obscures a very real parallel between the two in that on both occasions the man names and gives reasons for the name he has given. Lastly, the appeal to a 'formula' risks understating the substance of the action: naming is a significant thing, even where varieties of terms are employed. On this basis Atkinson's objections appear unsubstantiated, and Wenham's

---

[11] G. Wenham *Genesis 1-15* (Dallas: Word) 1991:70.
[12] D. Atkinson *The Message of Genesis 1-11* (Leicester:IVP) 1990:71.

judgement preferred that this is 'a typical example of a Hebrew naming.'[13]

3.3.5. The outcome then is that Genesis 2 does envisage headship between husband and wife, Adam and Eve. This then shows Adam's actions in Genesis 3 to be a refusal to accept responsibility and headship, but instead an adoption of submission to one who should have been submitting to him. Hence the criticism of Genesis 3:17.

3.3.6. One can thus see Genesis 3 as an inversion of the appropriate orders of creation. The serpent suborns Eve, who overrules her head, who defies his God. Athanasius accordingly rightly depicts the Fall as an undoing of creation. In this context Genesis 3:16, far from being a further punishment on the woman, is a preservation of the original creation order – a sign that marriage authentically continues in a fallen world (as Genesis 2:24 envisages), albeit under the shadow of masculine failures.

3.3.7. What this means is that a restored humanity in terms of its husband/wife relationships, would be marked not by *soi-disant* egalitarianism or 'mutual submission'. Rather a re-created marriage would be marked by the original creational marriage contours, namely complementarity and obedience within a loving relationship. It would be precisely the ordinal relationship of headship that marks marriage in the redeemed community before Christ's return.

3.3.8. It is therefore unproven that differentiation on the grounds of gender within the restored humanity is *ipso facto* a denial of the re-creation. It may be, when the differentiation in question functions to deny the sufficiency and necessity of Christ's re-creating work (as in the Galatian and Antioch cases). Yet in another case, that of marriage, the re-creation of humanity positively requires differentiation on grounds of gender, and it is the denial of that differentiation that imperils the prospect of living re-created lives.

3.3.9. The next question is therefore whether Scripture requires differentiation on grounds of gender within the church's ministry.

---

[13] Wenham 1991:70.

4. Texts bearing on women's ministry

4.1 1 Corinthians 11

4.1.1. 1 Corinthians 11:5 clearly contemplates women taking part in corporate acts of worship by praying and prophesying. The fact that men are dealt with at the same time (verse 4) strongly suggests that these are mixed-gender acts of corporate worship. Now it is clear that Paul is endorsing, or encouraging, the participation of women in such circumstances. Yet it is equally clear that men and women are enjoined by the Apostle to do these things in different ways in the Corinthian situation. Fee's analysis at this point is persuasive,[14] that a woman praying or prophesying unveiled is blurring gender distinctions within the Corinthian social context. This means that although the passage is upholding the participation of women in these respects, it is not simply doing so by saying men and women are 'the same'. Sexual distinctions remain, and are to be observed, although what counts as a distinguishing mark may vary culturally. It is therefore unwarranted to infer that this interpretation entails suggesting head coverings remain appropriate in the current English social context.

4.1.2. Obviously, some have felt some discomfort in reconciling this passage with 1 Corinthians 14:33b-36 and 1 Timothy 2:11-15. Yet it should be noted that the issues at stake in 1 Corinthians 11:3ff are prayer and prophecy. The gift of prophecy does seem to form a separate category within the New Testament list of ministerial gifts (separately listed in Ephesians 4:11, Romans 12:6-7and 1 Corinthians 12:29), and is not simply to be equated to the ministry of teaching, although both are verbal ministries. This pattern seems to continue outside the New Testament, for example in *Didache* 11 missioners and charismatists are treated differently.

4.1.3. This separate categorisation of prophecy helps explain an oft-cited conundrum, the place of Deborah and Huldah. Deborah and Huldah are both prophetesses (Judges 4:4 and 2 Kings 22:14) whose ministries fall within the scope of 1 Corinthians

---

[14] Fee 1987:511, 512.

11:3ff. Deborah is also described as judging Israel (Judges 4:4, 5) but it is dubious to see this as at odds with the provisions of 1 Timothy 2:11-15 or 1 Corinthians 14:33b-36, for what is at stake in these passages is the instruction of the mixed assembly of God's people and the decisive determination of the acceptability of particular material. The material in Judges tends to picture the judges as saviour figures (Judges 2:16) or those who fulfil the literal function of judges, namely determining civil disputes (see Samuel's description of his actions in 1 Samuel 12:3-5 where he depicts himself as an honest judge in the modern sense). It is then a bow drawn at a venture to equate the Old Testament judge with the New Testament pastor-teacher or presbyter. The functions are different, and the parallel therefore fails.

4.2   1 Corinthians 14:33b-36

4.2.1.   Fee aptly notes the absolute nature of the rationale for the prohibition.[15] His preferred method for dealing with the text is to reject its authenticity (in some manuscripts, these verses appear after verse 40), suggesting it is inserted by someone with a background in Jewish Christianity.[16] His principal difficulty apparently lies in making sense of the prohibition, given what has been previously allowed to women in 1 Corinthians 11:3ff, and he is surely right to think in terms of the need for consistency in Paul within such a short compass of material.

4.2.2.   However, Fee's handling of the textual question is unsatisfying.[17] For these verses to be an interpolation, they must have been inserted very, very early in the text's history. This is not a question of some manuscripts having the verses and others not (as with say, the ending of Mark's Gospel). It is a question of where a given manuscript puts these verses. They are there, it seems, in every known manuscript. Moreover, it is far from implausible that they appear after verse 40 in one manuscript tradition as an attempt to alleviate just the kind of difficulty that Fee finds. That is to say they were moved by one copyist because

---

[15] Fee 1987:705, 706.
[16] Fee 1987:707.
[17] For detailed argument see Carson pp 141-144 in Piper and Grudem *Recovering Biblical Manhood and Womanhood: A Response to Evangelical Feminism* (Wheaton: Crossway)1991.

they did not make sense to him in the position following verse 33a. It is therefore important to see whether sense can be made of them.

4.2.3. Carson follows a steady stream of interpretation[18] in seeing the context of chapter 14 as that of regulation of worship and in particular the circumstances under which prophecy should be weighed. This is the thing that is forbidden, the adjudication of the acceptability of a purported prophecy for the congregation. As such there is consistency with 1 Corinthians 11:3ff, for prophecy itself is permitted. It is the other step that is not. There is a further consistency in that 1 Corinthians 11:3ff rests on an understanding of the Creation narrative of Genesis 2, and in Carson's view this is the passage that lies behind Paul's reference to the Law in verse 34. Obviously this is also part of Paul's rationale in 1 Timothy 2:13 and 14.

4.2.4. Carson's synthesis is to be preferred here. He deals better with the textual evidence and produces an interpretation that allows consistency between 1 Corinthians 11:3ff, 1 Corinthians 14:33b-36 and 1 Timothy 2:11-15; moreover, he does so on a common theological basis that reflects Paul's abiding concern with Genesis 1-3. To an Anglican committed to the non-repugnant reading of various parts of Scripture, this must be attractive.

4.3   *1 Timothy 2:11-15*

4.3.1. It is, of course, possible to dismiss the text of 1 Timothy 2:11-15 as devoid of the Holy Spirit's inspiration and thus a text that can legitimately be ignored. Anglicans holding both to Article VI and to the first head of the Lambeth Quadrilateral, which assert the authority of Scripture, cannot happily do this. It should further be said that if this is indeed the method to be pursued in resolving the present question of women in the episcopacy, then this should first be openly acknowledged, for it raises the most fundamental questions of theological method, as well as issues of Anglican ecclesiological identity. Nor is it sufficient to observe

---

[18] Carson: p. 151 in Piper and Grudem 1991. He cites M.E.Thrall *I and II Corinthians* (1965. Cambridge: CUP); J.B. Hurley *Man and Woman in Biblical Perspective* (1981. Grand Rapids: Zondervan) and W. Grudem *The Gift of Prophecy in 1 Corinthians* (1982. Washington: University Press of America).

that factually within an Anglican cultural context there are theologians and others who do not endorse the primacy of Scripture. That is merely to confuse description with prescription: the point is the propriety of those views within an Anglican context.

4.3.2. For this reason the correct way of proceeding is to pose the question thus: given that 1 Timothy 2:11-15 is part of the canonical Scripture accepted as authoritative, what does it teach us to do? Two broad varieties of construction are discernible: (a) the passage contains a purely local or temporary restriction on what women may do that arose from a particular local situation within Ephesus; and (b) the passage contains a general restriction.

4.3.3. Within both varieties of interpretation there are different schools of thought. Nevertheless the vital point of difference between the two varieties lies in the place of the local. Now it is certainly true that 1 Timothy, like many other epistles, is occasional in nature: it originates in a particular question at a particular place and time. However, the occasional nature of some New Testament correspondence does not prevent it necessarily from having general application. Paul's hymn to love in 1 Corinthians 13 originates in the factionalism of Corinth. This context of origin does not prevent a more general application, for Paul solves the local problem by an appeal to a general truth, not a truth for the Corinthians alone. On this basis, we need to ascertain whether there was a particular local problem occasioning the passage in question, and if there was, whether Paul solves it by purely locally applicable or more general principles.

4.3.4. The case has sometimes been made that Ephesus was in some sense a 'feminist'[19] centre (a view finding some support from Markus Barth in his commentary on Ephesians), and especially of note in this regard is the cult of Ephesian Diana.[20] The kind of

---

[19] The term is used for convenience. There are obvious dangers of anachronism and over-generalisation – it is currently perhaps better to speak of 'feminisms' rather than simply 'feminism'.

[20] An example is R and K Clark Kroeger *I Suffer Not a Woman* 1992 (Grand Rapids: Baker).

'feminism' in question has been variously put, but the rationale is that women received the prohibition of chapter 2 because they had taught falsely.

4.3.5. This thesis of 'feminist' Ephesus needs to be tested against both extrinsic and internal evidence from the letter. In terms of extrinsic evidence, the patterns of Ephesian life uncovered by archaeology do not disclose a feminist city but a relatively typical one.[21] Thus epigraphic evidence does not disclose female control of the central religious cult of Diana: rather it was controlled by men (as were the municipal affairs of the city) and there were male celebrants in the rites themselves. As for the Diana-theology, it has been suggested that evidence for her as a fertility goddess is in fact lacking. The myths associated with her point rather to the notion of virgin-huntress. As for the multiple breasts in depictions of Diana, these lack nipples and start below where breasts normally do, and are also to be found in Asiatic representations of Zeus. This casts some doubt on the notion of an essentially matriarchal Diana cult based on the female principle as the originator and source of life. As for the role that the city's culture encouraged for women, again this bears a more typical Greco-roman stamp, with modesty and other 'domestic' virtues receiving praise. To this extent, extrinsic evidence tells against an Ephesian 'feminist' problem rather than for it.

4.3.6. Turning then to internal evidence, the following features are discernible. First, the teaching problems at Ephesus are not exclusively female. The use of masculine participles in 1:6-7 of the false teachers indicates that at least some were men. Secondly, if the prohibition in chapter 2 in fact relates to false teaching by women, this has already been covered by 1:3 – such a construction makes the 1 Timothy 2:11-15 passage redundant. Such a view also lies at odds with the terms of vv.11-12. The obvious remedy for false teaching by women is to prevent them teaching falsely, not to prevent them teaching, which is what verse 12 does. There seems little reason other than *a priori*

---

[21] The subsequent argument follows the persuasive work of S.M. Baugh 'A Foreign World : Ephesus in the First Century' pp 13-52 in *Women in the Church* eds. A.J. Kostenburger, T.R. Schreiner and H. Scott Baldwin 1995 (Grand Rapids: Baker).

assumption for taking the *didaskein* of verse 12 in a purely pejorative sense.[22] That is not its normal meaning, and would be especially inept given Paul's earlier use of *heterodidaskalein* in 1:3 to denote false teaching. Third, any reading of the Ephesian problem has to take into account the rationale Paul produces for his command, and to this we turn.

4.3.7. The justification for the prohibition of verse 12 appears in verses 13-14. These verses are introduced by *gar* (for) and this obviously indicates their significance. They take us back to the events of Genesis 2 (Adam was made first...) and Genesis 3 (Eve was deceived...). Paul cites them as a unit, and it is as a unit that they provide an explanation. It is therefore insufficient to see these verses as relying on female inability (that would not account for verse 13) or allegedly superior male intellect (again, that ignores verse 13). We are, though, taken back to the events of Creation and Fall. This in itself tends to dispose of a purely local and temporary understanding of the Ephesian problem with respect to women's roles. If the problem were Ephesian 'feminism', or the poor education of Ephesian women, then the rationale would not be on this grand and generalising scale. To produce a justification from Creation and Fall suggests Paul is producing a generally applicable principle.

4.3.8. It is no doubt true that Paul's words are allusive. Even so, a broad principle is visible. Having a woman teach and exercise authority over men in certain circumstances breaches what we learn from the events of Genesis 2 and 3. On the interpretation of Genesis 2 and 3 adopted above, it is possible to see how: Adam, created first, had been placed in a position of responsibility over Eve: he named her and should have been her 'teacher' as to what God had commanded. Instead he listened to his wife's teaching, who had previously been deceived by the serpent, thereby surrendering his own responsibility.

4.3.9. To this extent, having women teach and exercise authority over men symbolically continues the pattern of Genesis 3: it is the pattern of humanity organised in contravention of the original

---

[22] It is not sufficient to appeal to *authentein* as introducing a pejorative note, for it is not clear that the word necessarily carries such a tone.

creational order.[23] Conversely, observing Paul's principle whereby men have to assume teaching responsibility symbolically shows men rejecting the sin of Adamic irresponsiblity and embracing the original creational order. Paul's principle is, then, that the church manifests the re-creation of humanity by visibly adopting in symbolic form the creational pattern of Adam's headship over Eve.

4.3.10. In this way, the prohibition on women teaching and exercising authority does not detract from the unity of the re-created humanity. Rather it shows precisely how it is in contact with the original Creation, for what was marred, the inversion of relationship between Adam and Eve, is now set right. Instead, it is the *soi-disant* egalitarian case that faces difficulties over the unity of the new humanity. For it appears to advocate a unity at odds with that contemplated in Genesis 2. Ironically, the unity it creates is that of Genesis 3 – not the re-created humanity, but humanity in sin.

4.3.11. Verse 15 of 1 Timothy 2 continues this thrust. The pains of childbirth are *par excellence* a reminder of the Fall and the sentence Eve as Everywoman received (Genesis 3:16). It would have been easy to imagine that women continued fully under the effects of Genesis 3, or even to think that Paul's remarks of verses 13-14 implied some second-class status for women as believers. This is not the case: he affirms that women too will be saved, even though in childbirth the marks of the Fall remain (taking *dia* as denoting attendant circumstances [cf 2 Corinthians 6:7 and 8]), provided there is faith, hope, holiness and love – similar virtues, of course, to those men should show.

4.3.12. This leads on to the scope of the prohibition of 2:12. The context of chapter 2 is what Paul wishes to find in the community of faith (verses 1 and 8). This is sufficient to dispose of the idea that 1 Timothy 2:12 applies to civil government (female prime ministers or presidents, for example, as well as, in our own British context, the Queen considered in her civil capacity). To that extent, the teaching and authority in question is teaching and authority in the church over adult men, which disposes of

---

[23] It is occasionally thought that 1 Timothy 2:11-12 is dealing simply with husband-wife relations. The absence of any possessive terms (*idios, heautou*) tells against this.

the possibility that the verse covers teaching outside the church, acting as business leaders, or within the church teaching adult women or non-adult males.

4.3.13. While teaching and authority may not strictly be a hendiadys in verse 12 (the grammar renders this problematic), there is little doubt that teaching and authority are related concepts, since it is by teaching the Scriptures that authority is exercised in the Church and notably that Christ's headship is realised. Here the correlative material of 1 Corinthians 14:33b-36 proves illuminating: unacceptable authority is exercised by women in a mixed adult context when they determine what is or is not to be heard by the group in question. The point, then, about teaching and exercising authority is determining what is to be heard.

4.3.14. On this basis, whatever else an Anglican bishop does, he does in effect determine just this thing – either through the act of ordination or through his discipline of his clergy. Nor is it sufficient to say that many bishops exercise tolerance over what is heard in their dioceses, for this is determining by passively accepting that a particular position may be heard, determination by inaction rather than action, but determination nonetheless.

4.3.15. For these reasons, then, 1 Timothy 2:11-15 does prohibit women from the episcopate.

4.3.16. The argument is sometimes heard in response that this would also prohibit the Queen from being the supreme governor of the Church of England. If one cannot accept women bishops one should not accept the Queen in one's own ordination promises.

4.3.17. The answer to this is four-fold. First, the 1662 Accession Service does not involve the monarch in vowing to expel false teaching, as a bishop does. There are prayers for her salvation and her wise governance, but the latter relate to her civil capacity. Secondly, this argument mistakes the way that British constitutional law operates, which is that the monarch acts on the advisement of her ministers and not otherwise. In matters of appointment, then, the royal discretion is fettered. Dicey and Bagehot alike stress that British constitutional law cannot be understood adequately without a grasp of these conventions. Thirdly, the argument does not in fact provide a refutation of the view under discussion. Rather it is suggesting an inconsistency in the application of the principle. The principle itself, though, might still be true. Even if it were the case that the present Queen's position is in breach of 1 Timothy 2, it does not follow that this error should be further compounded by another breach of 1 Timothy 2. It is on a level with saying that if one has committed one sin, one should for consistency's sake admit others. Fourthly, if the argument of 4.1.16 above is seriously meant, then steps should be taken immediately to expel those priests and bishops opposed to the ordination of women to the presbyterate or their consecration to the episcopate. This would, naturally, involve an immediate rescission of the Act of Synod, and the church might give serious thought to making public that this is indeed its view.

5. Other considerations relating to the Episcopate

5.1. The discussion above has centred on an understanding of the episcopacy drawn from the New Testament material with its concern for the encouragement of true teaching and the prevention of false teaching, a perspective eminently present in the post-apostolic church. It is a view that classic evangelicals do find attractive, although, of course, others do too. Nevertheless, it is not an exhaustive account of contemporary understandings of the episcopate by any means, as evidenced by the list quoted in paragraph 270 of the 1990 *Episcopal Ministry* Report. Some of these further understandings also merit attention.

5.2. Prominent here is the notion of the bishop as a focus of unity. The material leading in this direction from Ignatius of Antioch has already been mentioned, but in particular one notes here the work of the martyr Cyprian of Carthage, especially the treatise *On Unity* and the *Epistle to Pupianus*.[24] In both works Cyprian derives the unity of the church from the single person of Peter, appointed by Christ, writing '...yet, that He [sc. Christ] might set forth unity, He arranged by His authority the origin of that unity, as beginning from one [sc. Peter].'[25] In consequence relations to the bishop are crucial for identification with the church. Cyprian writes: '...[You] ought to know that the bishop is

---

[24] Epistle 68 in the ANF collection Vol. 5.
[25] On Unity 4.

in the Church, and the Church in the bishop; and if any one be not with the bishop, that he is not in the Church...'[26]

5.3.   While by no means exclusively relying on Cyprian, this view that the bishop is the focus of unity, indeed constitutive of unity in some respects, provides significant influence on the 1990 *Episcopal Ministry* Report. That notion of unity is developed in three planes:[27]

(a)   unity within the local community;

(b)   unity between worshipping communities; and

(c)   unity between generations.

5.4.   In fact, the consecration of women to the episcopate provides disruption at every level the 1990 Report describes.

5.5.   In terms of unity within the local worshipping community, for the reasons given in sections 2-4 above, some will feel in all conscience that a female bishop does not unite, because by reason of 1 Timothy 2:11-15 and 1 Corinthians 14:33b-36 she does not manifest the new re-created humanity in its creationally ordered unity and its submission to God. Rather she will incarnate division.

5.6.   Several responses are possible to this. First, it may be said that this is a purely temporary problem. People will come round or leave. However, this has not happened over the ordination to the presbyterate. Certainly at the scholarly level, the arguments of advocates such as C. Clark Kroeger have in fact come under intensified criticism since the early 1990s.[28] For the argument to work, constructions such as the one outlined above have to disappear permanently from the field. This seems problematic.

5.7.   Secondly, perhaps more consistently, if Galatians 3:28 really does apply in the way outlined above and rejected, then the consecration of women to the episcopate is really about the scope of the gospel, and a denial of female episcopacy is a denial

---

[26]   To Pupianus 8.

[27]   See e.g. paras. 47-49.

[28]   See e.g. the review of *I Suffer not a woman* by A. Wolters in *CTJ* 1993 28:208, where at p 213 Wolters comments of the book 'its argumentation is a travesty of sound scholarship.'

of the gospel. If so, such people should be under the discipline of the church with a view to excommunication. There is simply no place for such people within the church. This would, of course, be at odds with Resolution III.2.c. of the 1998 Lambeth Conference, and some would see it as an issue of simple justice that if the dissentients are viewed in this way, then they should be informed of this, not least on the basis of Matthew 18:15ff.

5.8.   Thirdly, it may be said that the numbers with such consciences are insignificant and can safely be ignored. This is, of course, to concede defeat on the issue of unity. Unity is not on this basis all of the Anglican churches within a given diocese or area, but simply most of them. It also raises issues of what de Tocqueville felicitously calls the 'tyranny of the majority',[29] a theme that will be developed further below.

5.9.   Fourthly, one may rehearse the argument found within chapter 13 of the 1990 *Episcopal Ministry* Report that there is equally disruption to unity if women are not consecrated to the episcopacy. A male episcopate is said to incarnate division between humans. It is important to examine the scope of this argument.

(a)   It does not in fact provide a refutation of the point that female bishops do not act as foci of unity. It observes instead that there are unity problems with a male episcopacy. As such it does not lead to the conclusion that there should be female bishops, but rather to the thought that episcopal oversight should be exercised by those whom those ministered to can see as foci of unity. In the present context, that takes us toward differential episcopal oversight.

(b)   It does not deal with the possibility that a failure to see a male episcopacy as a focus of unity is, quite simply, wrong. In other words, a critical question here is what kind of unity is actually involved, a point to be raised later.

5.10.   For these reasons, the objection that a female episcopacy will not act as a focus of unity within a diocese is well taken.

---

[29]   De Tocqueville Democracy in America I.xv

5.11.   In terms of unity between worshipping communities, this too is fraught with difficulty, not only in terms of internal relations within the Anglican Communion, but also ecumenically. It is true that female episcopacy may well serve to cement relations in other directions, notably with ECUSA. The question then arises on what basis relations with one group are judged preferable to pursue rather than relations with another group. Why should proximity to ECUSA and like-minded Provinces be the apparent goal of Church of England policy within and without the Communion?

5.12.   In terms of unity across the generations, this too is problematic. It has been said that radical rupture from what went before is necessary, and the Reformation has been cited in this connection. In fact this is a superficial judgement. The quest of many of the Reformers was to recover the tradition of Augustine in his controversy with Pelagianism and to return to the Scriptures that stood at the head of the Church's tradition. In part they were reacting to the *Via Moderna* and the *ordo salutis* that this involved, precisely in order to recover their roots, not to depart wantonly from them. Accordingly, the Reformation parallel needs to be invoked with care.

5.13.   In fact it is just the presence in the biblical sources of material differentiating men and women within the redeemed humanity that presents the problem. Notwithstanding our indebtedness to the Fathers and the Reformers, *inter alios*, it is continuity with the generation of the apostolic church that is particularly telling. And it is just that continuity that the consecration of women to the episcopate seems to lose.

5.14.   Furthermore, this discussion of unity needs to bear in mind further material about Cyprian's conception of unity. Cyprian is often thought of as a bishop who stressed collegiality amongst the episcopacy. Certainly there is material in *On Unity* that can point in this direction. However, this judgement requires significant nuancing in the light of Cyprian's overall work. For Cyprian also deals with the problem of bishops who have apostasised. This is set out in the letter to the bishops and clergy of Spain about Basilides and Martial, two Spanish bishops who had obtained certificates of sacrifice in the Decian persecution.[30]

5.15.   Cyprian's words are worth setting out at length:

'Nor let the people flatter themselves that they can be free from the contagion of sin, while communicating with a priest who is a sinner, and yielding their consent to the unjust and unlawful episcopacy of their overseer, when the divine reproof by Hosea the prophet threatens, and says, "Their sacrifices shall be as the bread of mourning; all that eat thereof shall be polluted;" teaching manifestly and showing that all are absolutely bound to the sin who have been contaminated by the sacrifice of a profane and unrighteous priest. On which account a people obedient to the Lord's precepts, and fearing God, ought to separate themselves from a sinful prelate, and not to associate themselves with the sacrifices of a sacrilegious priest, especially since they themselves have the power either of choosing worthy priests, or of rejecting unworthy ones.'[31]

5.16.   Thus Cyprian indicates both that the laity of a diocese have an obligation not to consent to an unjust and unlawful episcopacy, and that bishops in other dioceses can intervene to point out this obligation – collegiality does not extend to tolerating apostasy amongst episcopal colleagues. Let it be stressed: Cyprian envisages the refusal of consent to unjust and unlawful episcopacy as a duty, not a mere option. The relevance here is that the interpretation of the Scriptural material above moves one towards precisely the view that female episcopacy could be characterized as unjust and unlawful.

5.17.   Nor is Cyprian out of step with other Fathers here. Origen in *Dialogue with Heraclides* is involved in the potential deposition of a bishop for heretical views (probably a species of monarchianism), while Athanasius in *De Synodis* is insistent that Arianising bishops be removed, and the Christological controversy of the 5th century likewise involves bishops commenting and adjudicating on the activities and beliefs of their peers.

---

[30]   Epistle 67 in the ANF collection
[31]   Epistle 67.3.

5.18. Further, this attitude is indeed to be found still within contemporary Anglicanism. Thus the Archbishops of Rwanda and Singapore write to the Archbishop of Canterbury:

'Since we believe that it is the Apostolic Faith that is the central bond of our unity in Christ, we believe that, in supporting the Anglican Mission in America [AMiA] and challenging the ongoing disobedience of the Episcopal Church of the United States of America [ECUSA] to the resolutions of Lambeth dealing with the essentials of the Faith regarding the Authority of Scripture, mission and even human sexuality, we are acting to strengthen our communion with one another.'[32]

5.19. To that extent it is highly pertinent that some regard unity under a perceivedly orthodox bishop and no other as morally obligatory, and that there are bishops in the Communion who share this view and are concerned to provide means by which this moral duty can be met.

5.20. It is of course true that other contemporary Anglican bishops do not share this Cyprianic/Patristic conception of the unity a bishop provides. Thus the letter of the Archbishop of Canterbury to the Archbishops of Rwanda and Singapore does not apparently advert to thought of Cyprian's epistle 67. What this underlines is at the very least that more careful thought needs to be given to the nature of the unity that a bishop provides.

5.21. Related to the question of unity on Cyprianic principles is another patristic *theologoumenon*, this time from Ignatius of Antioch. He suggests that the bishop is a type or icon of the Father.[33] While one might dissent from this judgement, one also must recognize its influence. It is to some extent problematic to see a female bishop as an icon of the Father. Symbolically she would tend to convey maternal rather than paternal associations. Yet the patristic thought with regard to the First Person of the Trinity is that he is essentially Father (by virtue of his eternal relationship with the Son). Maternal associations might well be thought to obscure this and to depart both from the economic

---

[32] Open letter to the Archbishop of Canterbury.
[33] To the Trallians 3.

revelation of Fatherhood/Sonship as well as the tradition of the church.

5.22. It would certainly be appropriate to consider directly the particular species of relationship given in Scripture and the Creeds rather than amend fundamental Trinitarian conceptions by the side door. It is in this respect a source of real disappointment that the relevant Reports spend so little time on the precise contours of Trinitarian theology.

5.23. Naturally, one possible answer to the consideration outlined above is that we must consider the First Person as parent (gender neutral) and that the bishop is then an icon of the Parent of the Son (or Child). However, there is some discomfort here too. The economy of salvation in the Incarnation is an entry into particular space and time and uses the forms of that particularity. While the language of Parent does not give rise to exclusively maternal associations, it nevertheless loses the specifically paternal associations (especially the father/son associations). In terms of the development of the tradition, a notable possible casualty here could be the monarchy of the Father, for within the framework of biblical theology of the family, father necessarily connotes the loving and final authoritative head of the family. Parent may well denote loving authority, but not necessarily its finality.

5.24. Of course, some (e.g. the followers of J. Moltmann) would not see the loss of the Fatherhood of God in this monarchical sense as any great loss. Others, following for example the Cappadocian tradition of Gregory of Nazianzen,[34] very definitely would, and would see the substitution of 'Parent' (in the Moltmann sense) for 'Father' as imperilling not just the monarchy of God, but the very principle that the economy of Incarnation gives access to the immanent Trinity. At that point it is not just the content but the very method of Trinitarian theology that is under discussion. This illustrates why the comparative paucity of discussion of this aspect in the relevant Reports necessarily handicaps present investigations to a very significant extent. This is not a question to pre-judge.

---

[34] Note here the Third 'Theological' Oration ii.

6. The issues of Justice

6.1 Introductory

6.1.1. It has been said that the consecration of women to the episcopate is a simple issue of justice. Since justice is such a fundamental biblical value, it is necessary to devote some time to considering it.

6.1.2. In fact, the issue of justice may be put in two ways:

(a) first, having decided for the ordination of women to the presbyterate, it logically follows that women should also be consecrated to the episcopate. *Like cases should be decided alike*; and (b) secondly, the concept of fair treatment for equal individuals requires that there be *equality of opportunity*.

6.2 Like cases should be decided alike

6.2.1. This argument invokes the principle that justice requires that essentially similar questions should receive essentially similar answers. It is to be noted that this is, so to speak, a question of the form rather than the substance of a particular decision. A legal system that, say, consistently favoured the rich would be open to criticism on other grounds of justice, but not this one.[35] Thus this principle does not claim to be a complete account of justice, but it is nevertheless an important one. In the English jurisprudential system it is reflected in the maxim *stare decisis* (stand by the way things have previously been decided), and is an aspect of what Dicey, following Voltaire, summed up as the Rule of Law: one may gloss it as the need in all fairness to ensure predictability and certainty within a system of rules, be they simply legal or more informal.

6.2.2. For this principle to apply in the present case, clearly one must decide that the cases of women presbyters and women bishops are essentially similar. That there is substantial overlap between the cases seems clear (as the 1990 *Episcopal Ministry* Report noted at paragraph 548), but there are grounds for seeing important differences in the case of women bishops (as the

---

[35] Note the seminal observations of Professor J. Raz in this connection.

1990 Report also observed: it declined to say that there were no differences between the cases).

6.2.3. The case for essential similarity is that bishops and presbyters are engaged in fundamentally similar tasks, notably teaching the truth, refuting error and pastoring the people of God. The most obvious difference is that priests do this within a fundamentally local context, bishops supra-locally.

6.2.4. Nevertheless this difference of jurisdiction does constitute an essential dissimilarity within an English context. The task of the bishop has sometimes been glossed as the pastor of the pastors, providing pastoral care and discipline and where necessary adjudicating on the acceptability of someone's teaching. The scope of this jurisdiction is a difference. The priest who dissented from the 1992 vote does not, on the view adopted here, necessarily find himself compromised by the presence of a woman priest in the next door parish. Within an Anglican polity he is not called on to exercise discipline over her. However, a woman bishop would necessarily be exercising the kind of jurisdiction over him that would be unacceptable for reasons of conscience. A woman bishop would be coercive in a way a woman priest is not.

6.2.5. Several responses might be made to this. One is that a sensitive woman bishop would not 'interfere' in this way. No doubt efforts would be made in this regard by a woman bishop, but it is still an unsatisfactory solution, for the New Testament evidence (as well as our own observation) suggests precisely the need for a supra-local jurisdiction such as Timothy's or Titus' in order to protect the people of God from false instruction. This value is sacrificed if a woman bishop, from the best of motives, pursues a policy of restraint. It is perfectly possible to have a tender conscience on the woman bishop issue and still need correction.

6.2.6. A second response is that this problem of coercion also existed over the decision with regard to women priests. Some might find themselves in a church where the vast majority were thoroughly happy with women priests and appointed one as incumbent. Is this not coercive, the argument runs. The answer to this seems to be, yes.

6.2.7. However, the scale of coercion in an English context is considerably greater. Given the geographical scale of England, it is a relatively simple matter to seek another church more attuned to one's own beliefs on this issue. This was the advice recently proffered in one parish to friends of the present writer who are dissentients from the 1992 vote. Emotionally, such a change can well be hard, but it is often physically straightforward. Indeed, it is a striking feature of current Anglicanism that congregations are not by any means simply the population of the local parish. Many Anglicans do now select an Anglican church on the basis of its churchmanship rather than simply its place as the parish church. Yet the geographical extent of a diocese renders such a choice far more problematic and changing dioceses for a priest is a far more difficult proposition than a member of a laity changing their regular church. The priest has to find another job. The prospective coercion is thus on a significantly higher scale.

6.2.8. A third response suggests that a female diocesan bishop could delegate oversight to a male suffragan or area bishop. No doubt the bishops of a diocese exercise in some ways a conjoint ministry, but the episcopal ministry in question would still turn on the decision of the diocesan not to intervene or be consulted. That too is an exercise of judgement, and the female diocesan remains the ultimate port of call for the diocese in terms of episcopal oversight. Thus, this in itself would not be enough. What would be enough would be a permanent delegation from the relevant diocesan, but on this view the male suffragan or area bishop would in reality be another diocesan, or something like it. There may well be much to be said for this approach, which amounts to an alternative oversight of a diocesan nature.

6.2.9. A fourth response would be that a female suffragan or area bishop would be answerable to a male diocesan. This too seems unsatisfactory, for in the present practice suffragans do have a genuine episcopal role, delegated as it may be. The objection applies to female diocesans and other bishops.

6.2.10. On this basis, the appeal to essential similarity fails: the extra degree of coercion involved over women bishops introduces a genuine difference between the 1992 decision and the present case.

6.2.11. Nevertheless, some may still insist on essential similarity between ordination of women to the presbyterate and consecration of women to the episcopate. If so, then consistency requires that similar policies be adopted for the dissentients over the consecration of women to the episcopate as were taken over dissentients regarding the ordination of women to the presbyterate. In fact, the measures for protection should be more stringent, given that the degrees of potential coercion involved are, as stated above, greater. If such protection is refused in the present case, then clearly this needs justification, if the appearance of oppression is to be avoided.

6.2.12. However, the question of the Rule of Law can be invoked in the present case in other ways too. A feature of the Rule of Law is its antipathy to retrospective measures. Some Anglican priests have been ordained and made their promises on the understanding of a particular kind of episcopacy, and the scope of their promises of canonical obedience now threatens to be extended in a way they did not intend.

6.2.13. Further, on any view the consecration of women to the episcopacy involves very considerable change. What is not immediately clear is precisely the method on which this change relies. In particular the proposed change seems to rest on a different weighting of the relative authorities of Scripture and our present cultural setting. If, as some say, there is a decisive tilting to the latter in the present instance, and our cultural setting continues to change radically, then it becomes increasingly difficult to envisage stability and predictability in the church's life.

6.2.14. To that extent, the very way the proposed change is argued for introduces principles at variance with the idea of the Rule of Law. For stability and predictability will have been eroded. Instead, the voice of the current majority will necessarily prevail, which again raises the topic of the 'tyranny of the majority' (de Tocqueville) and goes to the question of what properly constitutes Reception (see below).

6.2.15. The ecclesiological risks in creating a primacy of the current majority are in fact grave. They were of course adverted to in Tract 90 where Newman commented 'Religious changes, to be beneficial, should be the act of the whole body; they are worth little if they are the mere act of a majority.' Perhaps more significant is the work of John of Salisbury who noted the danger of ecclesiastical tyranny[36] in his seminal and influential work *Policraticus.*[37] A hallmark of tyranny in John of Salisbury's view is precisely the failure to accept one's position under law with a limited jurisdiction granted by God.[38] To the extent that majoritarianism can create the impression of *vox populi, vox dei,* John of Salisbury would see this as ecclesiastical tyranny.

6.2.16. Aside from Rule of Law considerations, one need hardly say that majoritarianism sits but unhappily with passages such as 2 Timothy 4:3ff.

6.2.17. For these reasons, the appeal to justice on this heading, far from simply endorsing the consecration of women bishops, if anything goes the other way.

6.3   Equality of opportunity

6.3.1. The point here is that persons of equal value should have tasks equally available to them, and that failure to make those tasks equally available is a denial of equality of value.

6.3.2. However, this argument needs to be significantly nuanced. As noted above, a Christian's value derives from the price Christ has put on them by his death. The same salvation for men and women does imply equal value.

6.3.3. Nor does value within the church become attached to the office or ministry performed (see above on 1 Corinthians 12). It is a secular conception of value that attaches value to the task performed.

6.3.4. Further, we do see differential allocation of roles, notably over marriage, without any suggestion that one role gives one party more value. Within this differentiation, some roles are closed. A female is not permitted to enjoy the relationship of being a husband with a wife, unless of course one repudiates the teaching of Scripture and the resolutions of the 1998 Lambeth

---

[36]   *Policraticus* VIII.17. He sees three kinds of tyranny: political, domestic and ecclesiastical.

[37]   Completed 1159.

[38]   Policraticus IV.1.

Conference. Nor is a male given the privilege of being a wife who has a husband.

6.3.5. Even outside the specific question of gender, equality of opportunity is not straightforward. Men who do not have the gift of teaching or who are recent converts do not fall within the specifications of 1 Timothy 3. Men who, whatever their other virtues, do not have the ability to refute false teaching do not fall within the admissible scope of Titus 1. Nor is this confined to religious opportunity. Natural qualities may rule out particular tasks. A strongly empathetic and trusting person, given to strong exercises of individual discretion is not ideal material for a traffic warden – nor are they devalued by not being apt for that particular task.

6.3.6. Nor do we find this particular version of egalitarianism obviously enshrined in the Trinity. To assert that it is found there, and to build from this a case for a female episcopacy on egalitarian grounds, is surreptitiously to smuggle in one version of Trinitarian theology at the expense of others. Once again it is necessary to note with regret that the relevant Reports do not tackle this fundamental question. Observations about the mutuality or perichoretic nature of the Trinity are welcome, but serve as a start for discussion, not an end-point. For mutuality and perichoresis have been explained in different ways: what kind of mutuality? What kind of perichoresis? Moltmann's? Or John of Damascus'?

6.3.7. For these reasons then, the appeal to justice on the grounds of equality of opportunity is unsubstantiated, and the appeal to justice fails under its second head also.

7.   Reception

7.1   Introductory

7.1.1. The previous fifteen years or so have seen immense effort spent over the question of Reception, notably with the work of the Eames Commission. However, in spite of the detailed nature of these earlier considerations, exploration of fundamental aspects of the question is still required. This will be done under the following headings:

(a)   the nature and place of Reception;

(b) the conditions for Reception; and

(c) whether or not Reception has taken place.

7.2   The nature and place of Reception

7.2.1.   Appeal has often been made to the Council of Jerusalem of Acts 15 as a precedent for Reception. This is far from being on all fours with the present question. There, the issue related to additional conditions for salvation, over and above the work of Christ, in other words an essentially similar issue to that faced in Galatia. In one sense the events of Acts 15 recall those of Acts 11:1-18 where Peter defended his actions with respect to the gentiles. In both Acts 11 and 15 the church was faced with what to do when God's Spirit was clearly and demonstrably present in gentiles without observation of the Law of Moses. In that sense Acts 15 relates to the evaluation of an existing fact, not the proposal to start doing something different.

7.2.2.   Further, the discussions of Acts 11 and 15 relate to the Law of Moses and its fulfilment in Christ. The present question relates not to the fulfilment of the Law, but to the observation of New Testament commands, given at a different stage in salvation-history. From a biblical theological point of view it is problematic to equate the reception of the Law of Moses in the New Testament era with our reception of New Testament commands.

7.2.3.   It should also be noted that the circumstances of Acts 15 demanded unanimity, for it went to the heart of the one Gospel by which the one God saves men and women. The present proposal has not always been presented as a 'Gospel issue'. If it is not, but a matter of conscience, then the appropriate analogy is Romans 14 and 15 which deals with the respect of conscience, and where unanimity of practice is not thought necessary by Paul for the unity of the church. Applied here, that suggests differential episcopal oversight to which priests could in good conscience submit.

7.2.4.   If, by contrast, the current proposal is to be treated as a 'Gospel issue' then it should be clearly stated that opposition to the proposal is heretical and requires the excommunication of dissentients. For this appears to be the apostolic practice of Galatians 1 and 2.

7.2.5. Nor does it avail to appeal to the example of Gamaliel in Acts 5:33-40. First, it is not clear that Gamaliel is being commended as an example, rather, in contrast to the apostles and church of Acts 11 and 15, he seems unable to discern the action of God's Spirit. Secondly, Gamaliel is not a recipe for initiating action, but for standing aside and seeing whether a given state of affairs prospers. To that extent, if Gamaliel is applicable at all on the consecration of women bishops, his example suggests continuation of the *status quo*, not its amendment.

7.2.6. It is sometimes said in this regard that Reception is seen in the case of the Arian Controversy of the Fourth Century. This, however, is to impose Twentieth and Twenty-First century categories onto that debate. Athanasius and his allies did not see themselves as arguing for the Reception of the Nicene Creed in the modern sense of Reception. Rather their point was that they were preserving through the Nicene Creed (and its derivative of 381 in Constantinople) what they had received through the Scriptures and the tradition. Only on these terms is the structure of argument of *Contra Arianos, De Synodis, De Decretis* etc. intelligible. In other words they saw themselves as bound by and under that authority, not able to choose whether or not to adopt it, as Reception so readily implies.

7.2.7. The foregoing paragraphs go to the central question of quite why it is that the consecration of women to the episcopacy has been adjudged a receivable question. For clearly on the rationale of 1 Corinthians 14:33b and 1 Timothy 2:11-15 adopted above it is not a receivable question. This underlines the central importance not simply of the doctrine of Reception, but of what issues are receivable. There are two broad possibilities: (a) all issues are receivable, including, for example, the deity of Christ. In this case, it is then hard to see in what sense the present generation is under the authority of either Scripture or tradition, a position significantly at odds with the view of Scripture, the Articles and the Lambeth Quadrilateral, as well as the church's self-understanding in earlier times; or (b) some issues are receivable. The paramount question is then the basis on which this categorisation of receivable or not is made.

7.2.8. Reception has not apparently been publicly argued simply in terms of option (a) of 7.2.7 above. Rather, Reception has implicitly adopted (b) above. And the basis on which an issue is adjudged receivable seems largely that a majority at the relevant assemblies deem it so. It is a decision of the majority.

7.2.9. It is at this point that some further careful reflection on the nature of majoritarian government would not be amiss. Earlier, mention was made of de Tocqueville's category of the tyranny of the majority. In a celebrated passage he writes:[39]

> 'In my opinion, the main evil of the present democratic institutions of the United States does not arise, as is often asserted in Europe, from their weakness, but from their irresistible strength. I am not so much alarmed at the excessive liberty which reigns in that country as at the inadequate securities which one finds there against tyranny.

> 'When an individual or a party is wronged in the United States, to whom can he apply for redress? If to public opinion, public opinion constitutes the majority; if to the legislature, it represents the majority and implicitly obeys it; if to the executive power, it is appointed by the majority and serves as a passive tool in its hands. The public force consists of the majority under arms; the jury is the majority invested with the right of hearing judicial cases; and in certain states even the judges are elected by the majority. However iniquitous or absurd the measure of which you complain, you must submit to it as well as you can.'

7.2.10. De Tocqueville's point is that straightforward majoritarianism leaves the individual quite without recourse, for all remedies have been controlled by the majority.[40] This creates the appearance of observance of due process and the forms of law. Yet as de Tocqueville comments of the era in which he wrote, the United States had successfully indulged in ethnic cleansing of native Americans precisely under the cover of legality and proper form. The point is the legalities and forms, the rights and remedies were controlled by the majority. In this sense de

---

[39] Democracy in America I.xv.

[40] For this reason it is anticipated that the Commission will not receive many submissions of dissent from the proposal. Dissentients may, sadly, feel that the process is guaranteed to produce a majoritarian result.

Tocqueville anticipates and instantiates the critiques of Nietzsche and Foucault. The latter perceptively comments:[41]

'As soon as one endeavours to detach power with its techniques and procedures from the form of law within which it has been theoretically confined up until now, one is driven to ask this basic question: isn't power simply a form of warlike domination? Shouldn't one therefore conceive all problems of power in terms of relations of war? Isn't power a sort of generalised war which assumes at particular moments the forms of peace and the State?'

7.2.11. *Mutatis mutandis,* Foucault here forces us to confront the question whether the apparently majoritarian decision to render this issue receivable is not simply a legal form behind which majoritarian power is in fact being pursued, but under the guise of legitimacy and fairness and democracy. It has to be said that a spirit of self-examination and self-criticism has not been conspicuous amongst the majoritarians. Yet the Scriptural lesson of 2 Timothy 4:3ff suggests this is highly desirable.

7.2.12. Nor is it an adequate answer to riposte that the dissentients likewise need to examine themselves. That is no doubt true, but in the nature of holding a minority position, one is constantly confronted by the need to justify both one's substantive position and even one's integrity in remaining within the church.

7.2.13. This will, of course, be dismissed by some as unduly cynical and uncharitable. Nevertheless, this perception is genuinely held, and it is almost always bad pastoral practice to dismiss the perception on the grounds that one does not agree with it. In this particular instance such a response merely heightens the hermeneutic of suspicion that Foucault advocates.

7.2.14. A more appropriate response is to seek to demonstrate that the suspicion is unfounded, and this relates to the question of whether the conditions for Reception are in place, to which we now turn.

---

[41] 122, 123 in 'Truth and Power' pp 109-133 in *Power/Knowledge* New York: Pantheon 1980 ed. C. Gordon.

7.3 *The conditions for Reception*

7.3.1. Resolution III.2.b of the 1998 Lambeth Conference enjoins 'Open Reception'. This picks up the language of the Grindrod Report (quoted with apparent approval by the 1990 *Episcopal Ministry* Report paragraphs 551-554). The Grindrod Report spoke in the context of 'open reception' of open-ness to the acceptance or rejection of the proposal to consecrate women bishops.

7.3.2. In the present context this presents an immediate problem, for, as observed above, some simply feel on the basis of the relevant parts of Scripture, or their understanding of tradition, that they cannot be open to acceptance.

7.3.3. Not unnaturally, this is likely to provoke strong reaction amongst those advocating the change. The feeling is that those disagreeing are acting in bad faith. This is not necessarily so, again for the reasons outlined above in relation to majoritarianism. It is not bad faith to refuse to play a game whose outcome is perceived to be pre-determined against one.

7.3.4. For, if there is a question about one party to the debate not being open to acceptance, there is also a question about the other party not being open to rejection. There are several factors which contribute to some suspicion about there being open-ness on the part of those proposing change on this issue.

7.3.5. First, if there is open-ness on questions of Reception, one sees it demonstrated where a party accepts a decision by the wider church with which it disagrees. In the present context of the Church of England's life, the reaction to the 1998 Lambeth Conference is scarcely encouraging. For the perception is that English bishops have either refused to act on Resolution 1.10 dealing with practising homosexuality or have positively repudiated it, as the then Bishops of Worcester and Newcastle are perceived by some to have done. The thought that arises is that if English bishops and others were sincere about the mind of the wider church, they would have acted differently in the wake of the 1998 Conference. Instead, they have created, perhaps unwittingly, the impression amongst some of appealing to the wider church where they have its agreement, but of disregarding it where they disagree. In other words, the doctrine of Reception is invoked opportunistically and not out of consistent principle.

7.3.6. Again, one suspects that the reaction to this account will be wounded outrage. This would be a mistake. While it may successfully dramatise the current episcopacy as the victims of misunderstanding and malice, a not un-enticing card to play in today's therapeutic culture, it fails to address the issue of the reality of the perception and the reasons which underlie it, but rather it will serve to reinforce the original perception.

7.3.7. The perception is in any event further fuelled by the thought that there seems to have been but little attention paid to the Reception of women ordained to the priesthood amongst those who originally opposed the 1992 Measure. The fact that there is debate now about consecration before adequate investigation of the Reception of the previous Measure further undermines the credibility of proponents as being genuinely open to the rejection of their views.

7.3.8. The present writer is well aware that the reflections of paragraphs 7.3.1-7 above will be unpleasant to read. However, it is submitted that the unpalatable truth must be faced that genuine open-ness does not exist on this issue on either side. Reception is therefore a fallacious category for resolving this dispute, not least because it is open to the charge of providing spurious legitimation (see 7.2. above).

7.3.9. If Reception is to be adopted as the appropriate category, then the preliminary work that needs to be done is

(a)   to persuade opponents that Reception is at least a possibility, and not merely to out-vote opponents by a majority that it is; and

(b)   to demonstrate good faith over the possibility of rejection.

The most obvious way of doing this in the present instance is to establish alternative episcopal jurisdiction. For, not to do this runs the risk of suggesting that the aim is to create facts on the ground which would prove 'irreversible': unfortunately this has the aroma of *realpolitik* rather than real principle.

In other words, unless the present damaging perceptions are addressed, the credibility of episcopal government more generally will suffer.

7.4 *Whether or not Reception has taken or will take place*

7.4.1. It is no doubt singularly difficult to establish that Reception of women's ordination to the priesthood has taken place or not. A number of routes suggest themselves:

(a)   has women's presbyteral ministry been disproportionately blessed, for example by highly successful evangelisation?

(b)   Has the perception of the church markedly improved as a result of the ordination of women?

(c)   Has the life of the church been enriched over and above what would have happened given the exercise of other ministries by women?

(d)   Have opponents of the original Measure found themselves persuaded?

7.4.2. On questions (a) and (b), the present writer is not aware of findings showing positive answers. This is not, of course, to say that these things have not happened: the evidence may simply be unrecovered, or the positive answers may be masked by other factors. Thus one legitimate response to a survey which tended superficially to show that churches with women leaders did not prosper was that the women in question were having to run 'ill' churches in any case. They might have done exceptionally well in difficult circumstances. Nevertheless, success in terms of (a) or (b) does not apparently seem to have been demonstrated.

7.4.3. In terms of question (c), in the nature of things this is extremely difficult to answer. That the ministry of some women in the priesthood has been greatly appreciated may well be difficult to deny. That some women have been less well-received is equally difficult to deny, and in the latter case might be attributable more to personality than to gender. In this sense, while the observation of the worth of women's ministry is well taken, it is more difficult to see this as establishing an otherwise unattainable success with respect to the presbyteral ministry. On this basis answers to question (c) would be necessarily of uncertain probative value.

7.4.4. On question (d), again evidence on this is not forthcoming in the requisite detail to make a responsible judgement.

Anecdotally, some in favour of the 1992 Measure are now against, and no doubt the reverse.

7.4.5. On this basis it is extremely hard to say favourable Reception of the 1992 Measure has definitely taken place.

7.4.6. It is therefore problematic to build a further question requiring Reception on another issue still requiring demonstrable Reception. Again, this is something that casts doubt on the attitude in which Reception is being proposed.

7.4.7. Finally, two questions about the possible Reception of women bishops need to be faced:

(a)   first, if Reception is proposed, what would count as the criteria of success? These obviously need to be framed in terms of criteria in which failure is possible, otherwise Reception is not a genuine process for it has an assured result. What would or should count as failure for a specifically female episcopacy?

(b)   Secondly, if there were failure, how would the consecration of women to the episcopacy be undone? What would happen to the women in post at the moment if such a decision was reached? If it is unthinkable that the proposal be undone, then again, this is not real Reception, for it has an assured result.

8.   Concluding reflections and Summary

8.1   Concluding reflections

8.1.1. The present writer suspects that the lines of argument outlined above will not persuade the Commission. As such the Commission faces the task of considering the place of dissentients within the Church of England. It seems quite clear that without protective provisions, certain classes of churchmanship, at least in terms of presbyteral ministry, will start to disappear from certain dioceses.

8.1.2. This process can be envisaged happening in at least two ways. First, as certain dioceses acquire women bishops, these will tend to become no-go areas for priests who feel in all conscience that they should not submit to female oversight. Secondly, such priests will be less attractive to train because they will be more inflexible in terms of location after training, an argument with primary application to those contemplating stipendiary ministry.

8.1.3. This process will be more, not less, significant ultimately for the laity of the Church of England. After the 1992 Measure, dissentients could no doubt often find some church in the vicinity that reflected their own views on the issue. This will be less possible when an entire diocese or episcopal area is under female oversight.

8.1.4. To this extent the effect in terms of churchmanship will be to eliminate progressively strong anglo-catholics and conservative evangelicals from various areas. This effect is not difficult to predict. It is perhaps true that some do not foresee this result, but such people should be acutely aware that this is the perceived likely result by those constituencies mentioned. Some in them feel that they are facing not just marginalisation, but elimination, albeit over a period. Faced with that, some will perhaps simply leave, as happened in 1992. Others perhaps will feel that they cannot faithfully accept female oversight, and will accordingly look for male oversight from bishops in the Communion who feel able, or even obliged, to provide it.

8.1.5. Naturally, the progressive elimination of strong anglo-catholicism and conservative evangelicalism might actually appear to be an incentive in some minds. If so, that agenda needs to be honestly and openly stated, and the church must weigh quite how pluriform it is prepared to be.

8.1.6. If, on the other hand, such elimination is not an intentional result of the present proposal, then the majority needs to give extremely careful thought as to how it can dispel the suspicions that currently exist. The Act of Synod at least points the way here. Suspicions might be dispelled by a process of differential oversight, which is not designed to phase out, although even here there would need to be an ability not just to ordain and discipline, but also to consider and adopt ordinands for training, as would happen with a geographically defined bishop.

8.1.7. The objection to the foregoing is that this would represent a significant rupture in Anglican church polity. The answer is that the current proposal will produce this in any event. The question facing us is what kind of rupture is least damaging. This at least has the merit of maintaining episcopal oversight within the overall frameworks of the Provinces of Canterbury and York, rather than the oddity of an Anglican Missionary Province to Britain.

8.1.8. Such a suggestion also has the advantage that it may preserve the reality of episcopal oversight. It is difficult in the extreme to envisage a female bishop establishing sufficient relations of trust with dissentients to be able to discharge episcopal duties. Apart from anything else, she also will be put in an impossible position.

8.2 Summary

8.2.1. The church must be considered in the context of God's economy of re-creating and redeeming fallen humanity. It manifests that economy, albeit now only in part. That manifestation fails if the church does not display Christ as her lord and if she denies his work in re-creating a single humanity.

8.2.2. It is male episcopacy that manifests Christ as head of the church and his work in re-creating and redeeming fallen humanity. Male episcopacy affirms the re-creative work of the Gospel. For the Scriptural and traditional position of a male episcopate does not violate the conditions of Christ's lordship or his work in re-creating a single humanity. Rather it abides by what the Scriptures say, and is in keeping with the following vital principles: that human value is found in redemption by Christ, not function or 'status' in the church; that the church is a diversely-gifted yet united body; that gender differentiation is introduced in Creation and preserved in New Testament teaching on marriage and sexuality.

8.2.3. The proposal for the consecration of women to the episcopate tends to violate both conditions of 8.2.1. above, for it sanctions what God through his Scriptures has forbidden, the exercise of decisive control of the teaching function by women in the context of a local congregation of believers which includes adult males. It is then female episcopacy which manifests not redeemed and re-created humanity, but fallen humanity. It is thus female episcopacy which denies the re-creative work of the Gospel.

8.2.4. The proposal is doubly serious, for a primary concern in the episcopal office is the preservation of true teaching and obedience to it, whereas a female bishop will be a visible symbol of a church's disobedience.

8.2.5. The traditional view offers a better exegesis of the relevant passages individually and a better and less oppositional synthesis of the material. It is preferable on this ground too.

8.2.6. If the episcopate is considered as a focus of unity, the proposal to consecrate women bishops will significantly hinder this.

8.2.7. The claims of justice in terms of the need to treat like cases alike or to ensure equality of opportunity are both misplaced in the present discussion.

8.2.8. The claims to the applicability of Reception in the present discussion are flawed by the oppressive use of majoritarian principles, in circumstances where neither side is genuinely amenable to Open Reception, and where in any event Reception has not been demonstrated to have taken place, except again by majoritarian appeals. Reception is not the right tool with which to address our current differences.

8.2.9. The present proposal raises issues of both Trinitarian theology and theological method that have not yet been fully aired. It would therefore be ill-advised to rule out theological options when the ramifications of this have not been fully disclosed and discussed.

8.2.10. If, then, the proposal to consecrate women to the episcopate proceeds, it should only do so after giving adequate safeguards for dissentients, which would permit them to have access to full episcopal ministry to which they can in good conscience submit, and which do not carry a built-in obsolescence.

MICHAEL OVEY

2003

Appendix 2: Biblical material on collaborative leadership

In his speech at General Synod, in July 2010, Professor Anthony Thiselton described how St Paul speaks in "we" terms of his own oversight of churches; he does not exalt his own status or authority over fellow leaders.

Paul and a Collaborative Ministry of Co-Workers – Professor Anthony C. Thiselton

The greeting in 1 Thessalonians 1:1 bears the name of Paul and his co-workers, Silvanus and Timothy. Paul is not a lone missionary-pastor, but exercises a collaborative ministry alongside others. A number of writers have recently called attention to this fact, especially W. H. Ollrog, *Paulus und seine Mitarbeiter* (Neukirchen: Neukirchener, 1979); F.F. Bruce, *The Pauline Circle*, (Exeter: Paternoster, 1985); and D.I. Harrington, "Paul and Collaborative Ministry", WTR, 3 (1990) pp.62-71. Paul also omits any chosen authoritative title, standing alongside others (fellow workers and readers) in friendship.

Origen (early third century) declares concerning the greeting "Paul, Silvanus, and Timothy": "Through this, he [Paul] is showing that where two or three were found as one, the Holy Spirit had elicited one sense between them and one speech ... They say and think one thing" (Origen, *Commentary on the Epistle to the Romans* 10: 7: 6; 'Fathers of the Church', civ, pp.270-71). He comes near to commending Paul's collaborative ministry. Ambrosiaster (flourished c. 375 - c. 384) writes that the three mentioned in the salutation and thereafter might seem to be overseers or bishops (episcoporum) in name, but the sense and the words are apostolic (*Ad Thessalonicenses prima*, p.212). John Chrysostom (c. 347-407) observes that in their common salutation, "He [Paul] associates him [Timothy] with himself." Yet, he adds, Paul places Silvanus before Timothy (*Homily on 1 Thessalonians*, 1; NPNF, i, 13, p.323). Chrysostom further notes, "Here, he [Paul] gives himself no title, not 'an Apostle', not 'a servant', I suppose because the men [the readers]... had not yet any experience of him ..." (p.323). He comments that this epistle was probably Paul's earliest.

Thomas Aquinas (1225-74) observes, "The Apostle ... does not mention his title, but supplies only his humble name" (Aquinas, *Commentary on 1 Thessalonians*, p.5). He also writes, "He [Paul] adds the names of two persons who have preached to them with him: Silvanus, who is Silas, and Timothy ... as is mentioned in Acts 16" (p.5). John Calvin (1509-64) comments that Paul introduces himself "without any title of honour". For the Christians in Thessalonica "acknowledged him to be what he was" (Calvin, *Commentary on Thessalonians*, p.17). Calvin further comments that Paul cites "others along with himself, in common with himself, as the authors of the letter" (p.17). William Estius (or Willem van Est, 1542-1613), Catholic Chancellor of Douay, repeatedly draws on other Patristic or Catholic commentators, including especially Ambrosiaster and Cajetan. Like Chrysostom, he notes Paul's absence of title, and follows Cajetan in suggesting that this is due to his deference or respect towards Silvanus. Silvanus is identified with the Silas of the Acts of the Apostles, who laboured with Paul and Barnabas in the gospel (Estius, *Commentarii in Omnes D. Pauli Epistolas*, ii, p.550). In the Post-Reformation era Matthew Poole (1624-79) similarly observes, "He [Paul] joins Silvanus with him, whom Peter calls 'a faithful brother'" (1 Peter 5:12), and compares his association with fellow-workers in 1 and 2 Corinthians, and at Antioch (Poole, *Commentary*, vol. iii, p.731; posthumously published in 1685). He also writes that Paul appeals to no title.

In the nineteenth century Hermann Olshausen (1796-1839) writes in his *Biblical Commentary on Thessalonians*, published posthumously in 1840, that Silvanus and Timothy, co-authors with Paul, had accompanied Paul to Macedonia, but had at first remained behind in Beroea, and then followed him from there (Acts 17:14-15). Timothy was sent to Thessalonica, but first met with Paul in Corinth (*Biblical Commentary*, p.383). Benjamin Jowett (1817-93), Master of Baliol College, Oxford, notes that Paul omitted the designation "Apostle" either because of his association with Timothy and Silas; or because he needs no appeal to authority (*Epistles* [1859], p.42). Timothy accompanied Paul on two of his journeys into Greece. He was with him at Philippi and Thessalonica, and probably when Paul wrote 1 Corinthians and Romans (p.43). Gottlieb Lünemann (1819-94) writes in the H.A.W. Meyer series in 1850 (third edition 1867). He considers that Paul omits an official title because of the "devoted love" which bound him to the readers (*Commentary*, p.18).

2 Thessalonians 1: 1, 2 carries an almost identical address and greeting. Like 1 Thessalonians, this letter comes from three people: Paul and his co-workers Silvanus (or Silas) and Timothy. The emphasis of the last twenty years falls heavily on Paul's collaborative ministry with fellow-workers. Frequently "we" and "us" are not merely an epistolary device, but represent a genuine plural (1:3, 4, 11; 2:1,13; 3:1, 4, 6, 7, 11, 14).

In my speech in General Synod I stressed that while many "demeaned" Paul's apostleship and humiliated him, this was never on the grounds of collaborative or shared ministry with others, but always on some other ground, for example his reluctance to accept payment as a professional orator. I cannot see that "sharing" ministry in any way "demeans" that ministry, unless we move from the New Testament to a later monarchical episcopate, to which even Paul does not aspire.

ANTHONY THISELTON

14 JULY 2010

Appendix 3: Biblical and philosophical material on collaborative leadership

In this Note it is argued that the central issue we need to address is not one of how to delegate power, but rather that of mutual equality in servant leadership.

Power, Equality and Collaboration: the key issues in the women bishops debate – Dr Vinay Samuel

1. Exclusive systems are generally seen as discriminatory and unjust. For example Rawlsian theory of justice posits its principle of difference along with the principle of equal liberty. The difference principle asserts that the greatest benefits must flow to the most disadvantaged. Offices and positions must be open to them under conditions of equal opportunity. More power should be distributed in order to achieve equality. Privileged positions must not be blocked off by discrimination using outmoded, irrelevant and unjust criteria. Entrenched discrimination must be rooted out. Unjust systems need to be addressed with fair procedures which oppose entrenched discrimination and promote equal rights.

2. Martha Nussbaum, from a Jewish background, understood Christian concerns better than Rawls, who was avowedly anti-Christian. She developed Rawls' view to give content to justice as capability and freedom. The focus on capabilities is important as these capabilities must be protected from disadvantages and existing disadvantages must be procedurally excluded.

3. So this viewpoint will see any argument to develop a 'collaborative' episcopacy as another attempt to continue exclusion. Collaborative ministry also raises the issue of power. How does an argument for collaboration relate to the issue of power when it comes to leadership? Who is arguing for collaboration and what are their power interests?

4. We need to turn to Jesus and look at the way he understood leadership without denying equality.

5. It is important to address the theological understanding of equality. Is equality in Scripture seen in terms of power, or in terms of humble service? A key text is Luke 22: 24-30. There our Lord spells out leadership in terms not of lordship but of service. So, in the Christian community we cannot be determined by the secular zero-sum game, which dictates that if you do not have political power you are dispossessed, and *must* seek to rectify this by accessing equivalent or countervailing power. It is this approach that leads to trading our hurts - the Anglo-Catholic hurt of being excluded in the future is trumped by the women's hurt over decades and centuries of exclusion. This is a hurt related to power and exclusion from power.

6. Our Lord's approach was to empower others through humble service – this in turn empowers us in his service. Otherwise the church is following purely political understandings, where even collaborative episcopacy would be suspected of covering up inequality. The priority of 'headship' of Christ and his church, or a husband and his wife, is the priority of responsibility of servant leadership. Jesus took the lead in washing his disciples' feet – 'Yet I, your Lord and master ...'.

7. Paul's use of his apostolic status is also instructive. He is as much an apostle as Peter. Paul legitimates his ministry by appealing not to the power of the apostolic position but to his calling to be a bearer, guardian and promoter of the Truth delivered to him.

8. When it comes to the power aspect of that position, Paul is clearly following Jesus' teaching on rulers and the exercise of authority that we have noted above. So his language is not of authority derived from a position but of an appeal based on his ministry. He prefers the servant language, with its collegial and collaborative sense, to the language of ruling with authority.

9. Episcopacy is not ruling but serving, resting assured that equality in Christ underlies it, and also that legitimacy rests not in the power of the position but in the sheer grandeur of the calling.

10. Collaborative ministry in the present debate is not about collaboration between equals. What did Paul imply in his salutation in 1Thessalonians? Did he imply equality in every area with Silvanus and Timothy, or equality in calling,

representing the Lord who sends them out? I do not think it implied equality in authority. But it certainly implied equality in legitimation. Silvanus and Timothy's ministry was as legitimate as his, and so they participated equally in the apostolic legitimation which he certainly claimed so firmly. By extension I think he saw their ministry as apostolic, just as his own ministry was apostolic, even if they did not minister together. So in my view it was legitimation without affirming a hierarchy. Hierarchy is primarily about levels of power, not of legitimacy.

11. Paul's limited use of his apostolic position suggests that he saw a distinction, between the legitimation to serve and represent the one who calls, and the power and hierarchy that can be part of the status of an apostle.

12. The language of power is integrally related to the power to rule. I see little of that in Paul. So, apostolic status was not about rule, even in enforcing order. The aspects of rule and authority developed and solidified later. We see a more functional view in Paul's writings.

13. I think this is at the heart of Jesus' teaching in Luke 22, where he warns his disciples that the status of leadership is not a license to rule but a calling to serve from below. Power flows from above and is expressed in ruling. For the disciples, however, exclusive focus on serving deals with the issues of power, by ensuring that the purposes of God are fulfilled, rather than being the expression of the status of a ruler.

14. In the current debate what is surprising is that women, who should be naturally aware of the conflict between power and equality, in practice are not willing to provide a better model than men have done so far. The legislation now removes any hint of inequality.

15. Women proponents should not now imply that, while equality is available, the accompanying power is not. The view expressed in the synod debate and its resultant vote was that equality must be expressed with untrammelled power without restriction. If legal provision is made for dissentients, then the proponents' view is that 'you have given us equality but have restricted our power.' Thus any apparent restriction on power is seen as a real restriction of power, for equality is only seen as equality if there is no check on the expression of its power.

16.   Women should have a better model than this. Surely the claim should be that we desire the position of bishop so that we may better serve. The 'no legal provision' view looks at equality as a position, rather than a capability. However, apostolicity is not a position for exercising rule and power, and therefore jursidiction. It is about the opportunity to serve with confidence.

17.   That is why we all, current diocesan bishops and those who aspire to that office, need to reflect on Jesus' teaching and Paul's practice, in order to develop a model which is true servant leadership, and which speaks powerfully to the question of power at the heart of any leadership in society today.

VINAY SAMUEL

JULY 2010

LATIMER PUBLICATIONS